W9-BGM-393

# PLAYBOY'S
# GUIDE TO CASINO GAMBLING
## Volume Two: Blackjack

# PLAYBOY'S
## GUIDE TO
# CASINO GAMBLING

### Edwin Silberstang

## Volume Two : Blackjack

WIDEVIEW
BOOKS

*Copyright © 1980 by Edwin Silberstang.*

All rights reserved. No part of this book may be reproduced, stored in a retrieval system or transmitted in any form by an electronic, mechanical, photocopying, recording means or otherwise, without prior written permission of the author.

*Manufactured in the United States of America.*

*Third printing*

Library of Congress Cataloging in Publication Data

Silberstang, Edwin, 1930–
    Blackjack.

    (His Playboy's guide to casino gambling ; v. 2)
    1. Blackjack (Game) I. Title. II. Series.
GV1295.B55S56      795.4′2      80-18975
ISBN 0-87223-637-4

*For Ron von der Porten*

# CONTENTS

# Contents

# Contents

# INTRODUCTION

Blackjack, or Twenty-one, as it is sometimes called, is the one casino game in which the player has an advantage over the house. Because of this fact, blackjack has become the most popular of casino games.

In order to exercise this advantage, in order to be a winner, the blackjack player must know how to play each hand correctly and know the correct strategy for the game. Not only must the blackjack player master this strategy, but also its deviations because of altered casino rules or the changed composition of the cards. All this will be fully explained in *Playboy's Guide to Casino Gambling: Blackjack*. In this book every player's option, including the now popular surrender, is dealt with in full, so that by the time you finish this book and understand its principles, you will be a winner at this exciting and popular casino game.

In addition to playing strategy, you will learn how to count cards, and be able to alter your bets according to the remaining composition of the cards you're playing against. There will be times when the deck or decks are favorable, in which case you will raise your bets. At other times, the cards will be unfavorable, and you will lower your wagers accordingly.

Casinos fear card counters, and for good reason. Counters are able to beat the casinos consistently and, therefore, casino executives are always on the lookout for the experts who can keep track of the cards. A chapter in this book is devoted to disguising your play, as well as other useful hints on beating the casino.

Finally, you will learn how to manage your money correctly while playing blackjack. Armed with this knowledge, you will find the casino bankrolls easy pickings, and our "hit and run" methods will ensure that you won't be barred from playing despite being a constant winner.

This is the one game that can be beaten, but the player must be patient! Studying and learning the correct strategies and then practicing them so they become second nature are essential. Only after mastering the strategies at home should the player bet with real money, but he or she will find, after taking the time and effort to study, that the newly gained knowledge will pay big dividends in constant wins and enhanced bankrolls.

# PLAYBOY'S
# GUIDE TO CASINO GAMBLING
## Volume Two: Blackjack

# I

---

# BASIC MECHANICS
# OF PLAY

## THE PACK OR DECK OF CARDS

Blackjack, as a casino game, can be played with one deck or two, four, or six decks of cards. When the game is played with one pack or two packs of cards, the cards are held in the dealer's hand and dealt out from the hand. When four or six decks are used, they are dealt from a "shoe," which is a wooden or plastic device built to hold multiple packs of cards and to allow the cards to be easily removed one at a time by the dealer.

Whether a game is played with one deck or multiple decks, the composition of each deck is the same. The standard fifty-two-card pack is used, each pack containing four suits: spades, hearts, diamonds, and clubs. Each suit contains thirteen cards: ace, 2, 3, 4, 5, 6, 7, 8, 9, 10, jack, queen, and king.

For purposes of blackjack, the 10, jack, queen, and king all have the same value, which is 10 points, and each of these cards is referred to as a 10-value card or simply as a 10. The other cards, with the exception of the ace, have as many points as spots on the card. For example, the 2 is worth 2 points, the 3 is worth 3 points, the 4, 4 points, and so forth, to the 9, which is worth 9 points. The ace is unique. It has two different values: 1 point and 11 points. The value players assign the ace is at their option, depending upon the cards they hold and their total value. For example, since no hand can contain more than 21 points without being a losing hand, if a player held 10–4–A, he or she would have to value the ace as 1. If this player gave it an 11 value, the hand totals more than 21 and would be a loser.

The suits have no inherent value in blackjack, and whether a player holds a 10 of spades or a 10 of hearts doesn't really matter. What is important is the point total, not the suits.

Whether one deck or six decks are used makes no difference as far as point totals are concerned. The same proportion of cards is present in multiple decks, and the rules of the game regarding the value of the individual cards do not change.

## OBJECT OF THE GAME

When we speak of the object of the game, we're discussing the situation from the viewpoint of the player, not the dealer. In its simplest terms, the object of the game is for the player to have a higher total of points than the dealer, as long as that total is 21 or less, or to have a valid hand of any total of 21 or fewer points while the dealer busts.

In other words, the player's object is to beat the dealer and thus win his bet at even money. Only when the player has a winning blackjack is he or she paid off at 3 to 2.

Other than having a blackjack, the player wants to have as strong a hand as possible and there will be instances when the bettor will hit a hand—that is, draw another card or cards—in an attempt to improve it. However, the player is always cognizant of the fact that when hitting certain hands, those between 12 and 16 as hard totals, known as "stiff" hands, there is a danger of busting.

This subject of hitting vs. standing will be discussed fully in Chapter VI on blackjack strategies, and tables will show players how to make the correct decisions at all times. But for now, players should be aware that they act upon their hands first before the dealer does, and so the danger of busting will be a constant factor affecting the players' methods of play, as well as their decisions.

Should a player and dealer both have the same totals, the hand is a standoff and neither wins. For example, if a player has 20 and the dealer 20, it is a tie and thus a standoff. The same holds true for blackjacks.

To summarize: The player wins if he or she has a higher total than the dealer—if that total is 21 or fewer points—or has a valid hand while the dealer busts. If the player busts, or has a lesser total than the dealer, he or she loses. Should the dealer and player both have the same total, it is a tie and a standoff (often called a "push"), with neither winning.

## THE ORIGINAL HAND

In blackjack, all the players and the dealer get two cards at the outset of each round of play. These two cards are known as the original holding or the original hand.

After a player is dealt two cards, he must total his points to see just how strong or weak the hand is. In certain situations the player might want to draw, or "hit," the hand to improve its point value; in other situations, the player might want to stand pat and not draw any more cards.

The following are some examples of original hands and their totals:

$(A = ace, J = jack, Q = queen, K = king)$

Q–9 = 19
5–8 = 13
10–4 = 14
J–K = 20
10–Q = 20

## SOFT TOTALS AND HARD TOTALS

All hands not containing an ace are known as "hard" hands and their totals are "hard" totals. For example, all the representative hands shown in the section above were hard totals, since none contained an ace.

Even when an ace appears in the hand, if it is counted as 1 rather than 11, the hand is considered a hard total. For example, if a player held a 10–6, hit, and got an ace, he or she would now hold 10–6–A or a hard 17, since the ace would have to be counted as 1, not as 11.

However, should the player hold 8–A, it would be considered a soft 19 since the ace is counted as 11 and the 11 added to the 8 gives a total of 19, a soft 19.

A soft total can become a hard total with an ace. For instance, if a player held an A–5, the hand is considered a soft 16, with the ace counted as 11. If that hand were hit and the player drew 7, it would now be A–5–7 or a hard 13, since the ace would now be counted as 1.

The advantage of a soft total, or soft hand, is that this hand cannot go over 21 even if hit. If a player held the highest possible soft hand (other than a blackjack) which is A–9 for a soft 20, hit, and got any card, even a 10, the hand has now moved to a hard 20, for the ace would count in A–9–10 as 1.

To summarize:

• A hard total consists of any hand in which there is no

ace or in which an ace counts as 1. Examples are 9–8, a hard 17; 10–6–A, a hard 17; and 8–4–A, a hard 13.

• A soft total consists of any hand in which an ace counts as 11, rather than 1. Examples are A–6, a soft 17: A–7, a soft 18; A–8, a soft 19; and A–9, a soft 20.

• A soft total can become a hard total when the ace value changes from 11 to 1. Examples are: A–6–10 has moved from a soft 17 to a hard 17; A–7–9 has moved from a soft 18 to a hard 17.

## THE BLACKJACK

Printed on most American blackjack table layouts is the statement "Blackjack pay 3 to 2." When we refer to this blackjack, we're not writing about the name of the game, but the hand that gives its name to the game.

Whenever an original two-card hand contains an ace and a 10-value card, this hand is known as a blackjack, and a player holding these cards is paid off at 3 to 2, as long as the dealer doesn't hold a blackjack at the same time. When both the dealer and the player hold a blackjack, it is a standoff, with neither hand winning. If a dealer holds a blackjack and the player does not, the dealer wins the player's bet, but is not paid 3 to 2.

A blackjack can be formed only from the first two cards dealt to the player.

The following are examples of blackjacks dealt on the original hand: A–K, A–Q, A–J, and A–10. No other holding forms a blackjack.

## BUSTING OR BREAKING

The highest total of points the player or dealer may have legally is 21. If either one has a total over that amount, he or she is said to have "busted" or "broken" the hand.

It is impossible for the player or dealer to bust with his or her original two-card holding, for the highest total possible on that hand is 21, or a blackjack, formed by the marriage of an ace and a 10-value card. The only time a player or dealer can bust is when he or she draws a card, or "hits," the hand in an attempt to improve its value.

The player always has the option of standing pat, that is, not drawing any cards to his or her hand, or hitting the hand. The player may hit his or her hand as often as desired, just as long as the player doesn't bust the hand by going over 21. For example, the player may have been dealt an original hand of 3–2, a hard 5. The player hits this hand and gets 4 for a total of 9. The player hits again and gets 6 for a total of 15. The player hits again and gets an ace for a hard total of 16. The player can hit again, but if the card drawn is 6 or higher, the hand will go over a 21 total and the player will have "busted."

When a hand has busted, it is an immediate loser and the player's cards and chips are taken away by the dealer. Even if the dealer subsequently busts, it would do this player no good, for he or she is now out of the game.

The dealer, on the other hand, is bound by rigid rules and cannot freely hit or stand pat. In casinos in Atlantic City and on the Las Vegas Strip, the dealer must stand on all 17s, whether hard or soft. In most downtown Las Vegas and the northern Nevada casinos, the dealer must hit soft 17s and must stand on all hard 17s.

If the dealer hits a hard 16 or below and gets a card or cards that make the hand total more than 21, the dealer is said to have busted and loses to all players still remaining in the game.

In some jurisdictions, the terms "bust" and "break" are used interchangeably, but for the most part we'll refer to going over 21 as busting.

# II

# PLAYING THE CASINO GAME

## SINGLE-DECK GAMES

When playing casino blackjack, the player is not only betting against the dealer, but also the house or casino which the dealer represents. The dealer is paid only a salary, but the casino reaps the harvest of its wins at the blackjack table. Therefore, if the player beats the dealer, he or she is in reality beating the casino, for it's the casino bankroll that the bettor is winning.

When attempting to beat the casino at this game, the player sits at a blackjack table. This table is slightly oval-shaped and covered with felt, which is usually green. The following is an illustration of the average casino blackjack table.

Betting boxes on the layout are available for all the players. Practically all casinos provide playing spaces for from five to seven players. Each player has a seat, and should remain seated during play. The dealer faces the players and always stands when dealing the cards.

At the table, the player can bet with cash but the usual practice is to convert the cash into casino chips. Although players can bet with currency, if they win, they'll be paid

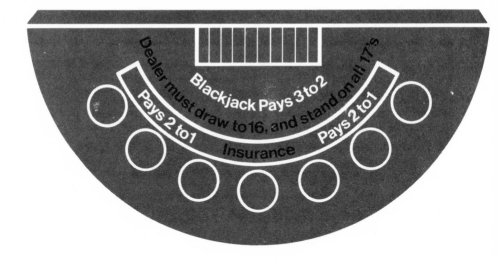

off in casino chips, which come in standard denominations of $1, $5, $25, and $100. The $5 chips are usually red, the $25 chips green, and the $100 chips black, although some casinos use their own color scheme.

Casinos prefer play with chips rather than cash. For one thing, the use of actual money slows down the game, since the dealer must carefully count and recount the bills, and is difficult because our currency is only one color—green. Dealers work more quickly with chips of different colors. Second, the casino realizes that players would play more freely with chips, which are but tokens representing money, rather than the money itself. It is easier for the player to put out four $25 chips in the betting box than to lay out five $20 bills.

At the outset of play, prior to the first round of betting, the dealer shuffles up the cards. After they've been thoroughly shuffled, the dealer gives them to any player at the table to cut. If one player refuses, any other player may cut the cards. Then the cards are restacked by the dealer, and the top card is taken off and placed either face up at the bottom of the pack, or face down into a plastic case at the dealer's right.

The removal of the top card is called "burning a card" and the card so taken off is referred to as the "burned card." This is a tradition of blackjack, and is probably done to prevent the first player from knowing the value of the top card and thus making a large bet if it is a favorable one, such as an ace. At one time, dealers in casinos showed the burned card to the players, but now that card counting is prevalent, this card is removed in such a manner to prevent any player from seeing it.

After the top card is burned, the dealer prepares to deal out the cards to the players, but first ascertains that each player has made a bet in the betting box. All bets in blackjack must be made prior to the deal, and if a player doesn't make a bet, he is not entitled to receive cards on that round of play. Some players, for whatever reason, sometimes refuse or neglect to make a bet and they are passed over by the dealer for that round of play.

The players facing the dealer are dealt cards in a precise, undeviating order. The player to the dealer's left gets the first card. This player is the one in the end seat and is known as the "first baseman." After the first card is dealt to this bettor, the subsequent card is dealt to the player in the second seat, then the third card to the third player and so on until the player in the last seat, the one to the dealer's right. In other words, the cards are dealt in a clockwise order, and the players act upon their hands in the same order, with the last player dealt to at the extreme right of the dealer. The last player is known as the "anchorman" or "third baseman." After the bettors act upon their hands in the same order as the cards are dealt, it is the dealer's turn, for the dealer always plays out his or her cards last.

The cards are dealt face down, the first card going to the first baseman, and then one card each face down goes to each player at the table. After they've all received their cards, the dealer gives himself a card, face down.

Then a second round of cards is dealt, also face down, except that the dealer turns one of the cards face up. This card is known as the "upcard" and will be referred to in the future as the upcard or dealer's card.

The players see one of the dealer's cards, but the dealer sees none of theirs. However, it wouldn't matter if he saw both of their cards, for the play of his own hand is rigidly bound by rules dealing not with the players' hands or totals, but with his own.

It also doesn't matter whether the cards are dealt face up or down to the players, but the tradition at single-deck and double-deck (and, in some instances, four-deck) games is to deal the players' cards face down. It gives the bettors a feeling of secretly playing their cards, which are unseen by either the dealer or the other players. This tradition favors only the weaker players, since experts and card counters would prefer to see all the players' cards dealt face up, for the count would be that much easier. Many poor players, who constantly make mistakes in playing out their hands, fear open games where their terrible play will be scrutinized by other players and perhaps commented upon.

In many multiple-deck games, the cards are dealt face up to all players. This not only speeds up the game—since players don't have to pick up and examine their cards and then hold them, waiting to make a decision—but also prevents cheating. Cheating can be accomplished successfully only when players handle the cards, but when cards are dealt face up, they need not be touched by the players except in certain situations, such as when they're splitting cards.

Otherwise, when hitting or standing, all the players have to do is point to the cards for a hit, and wave one hand over their cards if they wish to stand pat. This prevents card cheats from removing unfavorable cards in the decks, such as 3s, 4s, 5s, and 6s, and replacing them with 10s and aces. This is done where four- or six-deck games are played and the cards dealt face down are removed and replaced by scam artists who are called "muckers" or "hand muckers." When cards are dealt face up, these cheats can no longer constantly touch and manipulate the cards, and cheating is kept down to a minimum.

Cards can't be replaced in the single-deck game, even when they're dealt face down because there is one of each card in the deck, and a cheat who attempts to put in a couple of extra aces would find himself embarrassed by two aces of spades showing up at one time. In four- and six-deck games, there are many duplicate cards, and two kings of hearts wouldn't attract any attention.

In a single-deck game, after all the players have received two cards face down, and after the dealer has received two cards, one face up (the upcard) and one face down (the hole card), the dealer waits for the players to act upon their hands in those situations in which he has not dealt himself a blackjack. The first baseman acts first and gets the dealer's attention.

If the first baseman is satisfied with the total and wishes to stand pat, this player slides the cards under the chips in the box. To indicate the desire for another card, the player scrapes the two cards on the felt surface toward his or her body. This motion is a universal casino signal to draw another card. The scraping motion, rather than any verbal direction, is used for a good reason. Scraping of cards is an affirmative act, not an ambiguous one. If a player requests another card orally, he might be misunderstood, and a player who asks a question of the dealer that sounded like a request for another card would be dealt an unwanted card, which would lead to a disagreement and possibly an argument. There is generally a lot of noise and commotion in any casino, and sometimes with the noise from the slot machines, a small band playing in a lounge, and the general sounds of a large crowd, it's impossible to hear oneself talk, let alone make sensible or understood requests.

Players who hit their hands and bust are required to turn their cards face up immediately and lose them, along with their bets. If they don't do this, they will be told firmly by the dealer to do it next time.

Players should also turn up their cards immediately if they have a blackjack, so that the dealer can pay them off at 3 to 2 and collect the cards, unless the dealer, too, has blackjack, which is a standoff, or a "push."

Players should also turn over their cards if they surrender the hand, double down, or split a pair. All this will be fully explained in the next chapter dealing with the players' options.

After the first baseman acts upon his or her hand, it is the second player's turn, then the third player all the way to the third baseman, the last player at the table. After this last bettor acts upon his or her hand, the dealer turns over his hole card, and for the first time the players see the dealer's full total. According to the rigid rules of the casino, the dealer acts upon and plays out his hand. The dealer does this without looking at or caring about the players' totals. In casinos on the Las Vegas Strip and in Atlantic City, the dealer must stand on all 17s, soft or hard, and hit to all hands 16 or below. In northern Nevada and downtown Las Vegas, the dealer will stand only on hard 17s, and hit all soft 17s and hands of 16 or below.

That is all the dealer can do with the hand: If the total is above 17 he or she must stand. It doesn't matter if the dealer knows that all the players have 20 and he or she has 18; the dealer must still stand. Likewise, if the players have totals of 12, 13, 14, or 15, and the dealer has 16, the dealer must still hit the hand, even though, by standing, he could beat all the players.

Although there are other options available to the players, in our illustrative hands played in a casino, we'll stick to the hitting and standing plays. Let's assume we're at a casino playing single-deck blackjack. There are five players at the table, and as we begin this scenario, the cards have been freshly shuffled, a player has cut them, and the dealer has already burned the top card and is ready to deal out the cards to the players. Each player has made a bet in his or her betting box.

Following are the original hands dealt to the bettors:

( A = ace, K = king, Q = queen, J = jack )

| | |
|---|---|
| Player A | 6–J |
| Player B | 4–A |
| Player C | A–10 |
| Player D | J–K |
| Player E | 2–3 |
| Player F | 9–8 |
| Dealer | ?–Q |

The ? stands for the dealer's hole card, which is not seen by the players, but which the dealer has examined and which does not give him a blackjack. The bettors will now have to act upon their hands guided by two factors: their own totals and the dealer's upcard, the queen.

Player A holds 6 and jack, a hard 16. This is the worst of the "stiff hands." A stiff hand can be defined as any hard total from 12 through 16, which, if hit, is in danger of busting. Player A is worried about the dealer's queen as well as his own hard 16. If he hits the hand, he realizes that any card 6 or higher will bust his hand. However, he also is aware that the dealer has a very good chance of holding a 7 or higher card in the hole, and thus, if he doesn't hit his own hand, the dealer might easily win by forfeit.

Player A, in this predicament, decides to hit his hand. He scrapes the cards against the felt surface toward his body and the dealer responds by dealing a card off the top of the pack. This card and all subsequent cards drawn to hands are dealt face up. The dealer gives Player A a 7. Unfortunately for Player A, this card gives his hand a total of more than 21, and so he has busted and lost. Player A turns over his cards, and his bet and cards are immediately taken away from him by the dealer. Player A is now out of the game for this round of play, and even if the dealer should subsequently bust, it wouldn't help Player A at all. That is one of the great advantages that the dealer has in blackjack, acting upon his own hand last. This forces the players to make decisions, sometimes losing ones, before the dealer even reveals his or her total to the bettors.

Player B holds 4 and ace, for a soft total of 15. No matter what card Player B gets if she hits, she cannot bust her hand, for no soft total can ever bust. She scrapes her cards and gets 8. Now she holds 4–A–8, or a hard total of 13. The ace is now counted as 1 in her hand, and it is no longer a soft hand. Player B, holding a stiff hand now, feels that she can hit again to improve the hand. She knows the 13 won't win unless the dealer busts, and the dealer, with the queen showing, has a good chance of standing pat with a total of 17 or more. So she scrapes the cards again for another hit and gets 7, for a 20 total. This gives her a strong hand, and she pushes her original two cards under her wager, signifying to the dealer that she is now standing pat.

Player C has been dealt a blackjack. He happily turns over his cards and is paid 3 to 2 for his bet. His cards are removed at once by the dealer.

Player D has a strong total of 20 with the jack and king.

A card can't sanely be drawn to this total, so Player D pushes her cards under her wager to show that she is standing pat with her hand.

Player E has a hard 5 on a 2–3. She can afford to hit her hand, for her total is so low that no one card can bust her hand. She scrapes for a hit and gets 5, giving her a hard 10. Again, she scrapes for a hit, for there is no card that can bust the hand. The next card she gets is 9, giving her a hard 19, a fairly strong total. Satisfied now, Player E pushes her cards under her bet chips to indicate that she is standing pat.

Player F holds 9–8, a hard 17. This hand isn't very strong, but it is too dangerous to hit, for there are nine cards capable of busting it, so he stands pat by shoving his cards under the bet chips.

At this point, all the players have acted upon their individual hands, and it is the dealer's turn to play out his cards. He turns over his hole card, which is 9, giving him a hard total of 19. Under casino rules, he must stand, and now he prepares to examine the players' cards.

The dealer turns over the bettors' hands one at a time, starting with Player B, since Player A has busted and is out of the round. (In some casinos the payoffs start off in reverse order.)

Player B has 20, a higher total than the dealer and is paid off at even money. Player D, also with 20, is paid off at even money. Player E has 19, and this ties the dealer, so no money passes hands, since it is a standoff. Player F loses his bet, for his total of 17 is below the dealer's 19, and his chips are removed by the dealer. Now all the players' discards are added to the burned card, and the players make fresh bets in their respective betting boxes, as the dealer prepares to deal out another round of cards.

## DOUBLE-DECK GAMES

Double-deck games, in which the two decks of cards are held by hand by the dealer, are played in the same manner as single-deck games. The cards are dealt face down and the players scrape on the table for hits, and tuck their original cards under the bet chips when they stand pat.

## FOUR- AND SIX-DECK GAMES

Whether the game is dealt with one or two decks held by hand or four or six decks dealt out of a shoe doesn't affect the casino rules. However, there is a slight difference in style of play affecting hitting and standing procedures in certain cases.

In all four- and six-deck games, a shoe is used to facilitate the dealing, since it would be too cumbersome for the dealer to hold 208 or 312 cards in one hand. The shoe is a plastic or wooden box built to hold multiple decks securely and to allow the dealer to slide the cards out easily one at a time.

First, all the cards are shuffled and cut. The cut is done by a player inserting a plastic marker card somewhere in the decks. Next, the dealer inserts a marker card about three quarters of the way into the decks and puts the cards in the shoe to the left of the dealer. After a number of rounds of play when the marker appears, the remaining cards are taken out of the shoe and put together with the previous discards, and all the cards are then reshuffled. Before dealing, the dealer always burns the top card by sliding it out of the shoe and placing it in a plastic box on the right, where all the other discarded cards also go.

Multiple decks dealt out of a shoe make the game faster and easier for both dealers and casinos.

The single-deck game requires frequent reshuffling, slowing up the action. Generally, with a full table, no more than two rounds are played out before the cards have to be gathered together and shuffled up by the dealer. While the cards are being shuffled, there is no betting and no money changes hands. Reshuffling is a necessity, but a waste of time, as far as the casino is concerned. In a four- or six-deck game, there are many more rounds of play before reshuffling is necessary. This means a faster and more profitable game for the house, all other factors being equal.

Before card counting became popular, the single-deck game was the casino standard, and most decks were dealt down to the bottom card before the cards were reshuffled. Now, to thwart card counters and to prevent "end play," that is, the memorization of the last cards in the deck by a card counter, the decks are generally "broken" when about half the cards are used up in play.

The future seems to belong to the multiple decks. Many casinos, such as the Dunes in Las Vegas, which formerly had only single-deck games, have shifted to four decks dealt out of a shoe. All the casinos springing up in Atlantic City feature four- and six-deck games. No plans are being made in Atlantic City for single-deck games to be used in the future. Casinos in northern Nevada still have most of the blackjack games played with single decks, but their rules are not as favorable to the players as they are in Las Vegas and Atlantic City.

When multiple decks are used, it has been the custom of the majority of casinos employing shoes to deal the cards face up to the players. The casinos do this for speed and also to prevent cheating, for only when the players double down or split pairs do they touch their cards. When players want a hit, instead of scraping the cards, they point to them with the index finger. Some bettors crook their index finger, but it is best simply to point at the cards. When the player is satisfied with his total, he waves his hand, palm down, over the cards, indicating to the dealer that he is standing pat. These are universally accepted signals when cards are dealt open, or face up.

These are the only differences between the single- and the multiple-deck games that the bettor will encounter. The rules of play which might differ and vary have more to do with casino or jurisdictional policy than whether or not the game is a single-deck one. It is not the number of decks that determines the rules of play; some casinos feature both single- and four-deck games at their tables with the same rules governing both.

# III

# PLAYER'S OPTIONS

Although dealers in casino blackjack have no options open to them and must abide by the rigid rules of the casino where they work, players have several important options available to them. All of the options discussed below have some value and are favorable to the bettors when used correctly. The best use of these options are found in Chapter VI, dealing with winning strategies.

The following are the player's options:

• *Hitting or standing.* The player may hit, or draw additional cards to improve the point total without restriction, as long as the total doesn't exceed 21, in which case the player will have busted the hand and lost.

The player may also stand pat on any total, no matter how weak it is, and refuse to hit a hand. The player may hit or stand according to the correct strategy for playing the hand, and is not bound by the same rigid rules the dealer must follow. This option is available in all casinos and can be used very favorably by the player.

• *The ace can be counted as 1 or 11.* The player may form the best hand by counting the ace as 1 or 11, whichever will benefit him more. This option is very valuable and is available in all casinos.

• *Splitting pairs.* The player may split any pair in the original hand, and play out each split card as the base of a new hand. Pairs are defined as cards of the same rank, such as 2s, 3s, 6s, 8s, or 9s. All 10-value cards are considered as pairs of the same rank, and if a player is dealt a jack and a king, these may be split, as well as a 10 and a queen. There is a different rule for aces, which is covered in the next section.

When the player splits a pair, he or she makes another bet on the layout equal to the original bet on the hand. For example, if the wager is $10 and the bettor is dealt a pair of 8s, the player would have to make an additional $10 bet, so that each 8 would be played as separate hands with $10 riding on the individual 8s.

When the original cards are dealt face down, the player turns over the pair and splits them, making the additional bet. When cards are dealt face up, the player separates the pair and makes an additional bet. Thereafter, as new cards are dealt to each split card, they're dealt face up.

The player may hit each separated card as often as desired to form the best hands. For example, if the player split 8s, the two new hands might look like this: first 8: 8–4–2–5; second 8: 8–K.

When 10-value cards are split, the same rules apply. Suppose the player were dealt a jack and a king and split them. The two new hands might look like this: jack: J–4–6; king: K–9.

When 10-value cards are split and an ace is dealt to either 10, the new hand does not form a blackjack, but merely a 21 total and is paid off at even money if won. A blackjack can be formed only on the original two cards in the player's hand.

• *Splitting aces.* Aces may also be split, but the general rule is that only one additional card may be dealt to each ace to form the best hand. For example, if a player split aces and received 2 on the first ace, he would have no chance to draw another card, but would be stuck with this poor total. If the other ace received a 3, he would have two very weak hands, but the player could do nothing about it.

Aces dealt on aces usually cannot be resplit, except in a few casinos such as the Four Queens and Horseshoe Club in downtown Las Vegas. Otherwise, the player is stuck with an ace upon an ace, a weak hand wasting two aces.

When splitting aces, the bettor turns over the cards and receives one card on each ace, dealt face down in casinos where all cards are dealt face down. In casinos where cards are dealt face up, the new cards are dealt face up.

In casinos where aces can be resplit, the cards are dealt face up so that the player has the option of separating another ace if it is dealt to a split ace. To do this, an additional bet would have to be made on the third ace.

The rules are strict about splitting aces because the ace is valued at 11 points and is strong enough to take only one additional card and still win most of the time, since a 10 on the ace forms a 21 total.

• *Resplitting pairs.* Except for Atlantic City casinos, where pairs, once split, cannot be resplit, in practically all other casinos pairs (other than aces) can be resplit as often as necessary.

For example, suppose the bettor were dealt two 9s. The player splits them and gets the following: first 9: 9–3–6; second 9: 9–9.

Since the third 9 was dealt onto an individual 9, the second hand can be resplit, and the bettor has three hands to play out instead of two. Of course, the player must make another equal bet on the third 9.

However, in the following situation, the 9s could not be resplit: first 9: 9–3–6; second 9: 9–2–9.

The third 9 was dealt to the 9–2, not to an individual 9, and therefore could not be split.

The best strategy to follow in splitting and resplitting pairs is this: If the first split was worthwhile, then all resplitting of the same pairs is also worthwhile. Splitting pairs is very favorable to the player when done correctly. Re-splitting pairs and especially aces is also a very valuable option.

• *Doubling down.* In all casinos the player has the option of doubling the original bet on the first two cards. However, the rules of doubling down differ from jurisdiction to jurisdiction. In Las Vegas and Atlantic City, the bettor may double the wager on any two-card total in the original hand. In northern Nevada, doubling down is usually restricted to original totals of 10 or 11.

In order to double down, a player does not have to double the original bet. The player may make an additional bet up to the amount of the original wager. For example, if a player had bet $50 on the original hand, and doubled down, the new bet is up to $50 as an additional wager on the hand. It always pays to bet the maximum amount, however, because doubling down is a very valuable option open to the player, and wins most of the time.

In casinos where cards are dealt face down, the bettor turns over the hand to double down and makes an additional bet next to the original wager. In casinos where cards are dealt face up, the bettor simply makes an additional wager, also informing the dealer that he or she is doubling down.

After doubling down, the player is entitled to only one additional card, and no more. That is the basic risk of doubling down, but the maneuver is still worthwhile, for most double downs are made with totals such as 10 or 11, which are ideal cards to form a solid hand. Even when double downs are made on totals such as soft 14s, for example (see Chapter VI on winning strategies) these double downs are made when the dealer shows a stiff card as the upcard, and the chances are in the player's favor.

This option, as we have stated, is a very valuable one. Where casinos restrict the doubling down to only hard totals of 10 or 11, rather than on any original holding, the player is at a disadvantage. It is more favorable to play at a casino where any original hand may be doubled down, no matter what the total.

• *Doubling down after splitting pairs.* Some casinos, notably the Atlantic City ones, allow players to double down after splitting a pair. This procedure works as follows: Let's assume that the bettor has split a pair of 9s against the dealer's 6, which is a very good move. On the first 9, the player gets 2, making the new hand 9–2 or 11. The player may now double down this hand in casinos that allow this option. Should the player double down, he or she is bound by the rules of doubling down, having to make a bet up to the amount of the original bet on the hand and will receive only one card on the doubled-down hand. This is a very favorable option, rarely allowed outside Atlantic City casinos, though some clubs on the Las Vegas Strip do permit it.

• *Surrender.* When exercising this option, the player must give up the hand and half the original bet, rather than play out the hand or act upon it. In essence, the player is "surrendering" both the hand and half the bet.

This option cannot be used once the player has acted upon the hand in any manner, such as hitting, splitting pairs, or doubling down. Only before the bettor has acted upon the original two cards dealt is the option valid. This is a valuable option, and will be fully discussed in the section on surrender in Chapter VII, together with the strategies used with this option.

To surrender a hand where cards are dealt face down, the player must turn over the hand and announce the surrender. Then half the wager and the two cards are taken away by the dealer. The same is true where the cards are dealt face up, except that the player doesn't touch the cards. When surrendering, the player shouldn't touch the chips, but should let the dealer remove the correct amount.

Casino personnel frown on players touching their wagers in the betting box anytime after the cards have been dealt.

• *Insurance.* Whenever the dealer has an ace as the up-card, in practically all casinos, players are permitted an insurance bet. They may bet half their original wagers that the dealer has a 10-value card in the hole to make a black-jack, and if the dealer has a blackjack, the players are paid off at 2 to 1.

If the dealer doesn't have a blackjack, the insurance bets are lost, and the game goes on as before. In all but the At-lantic City casinos, the insurance bet is won or lost before the players act upon their hands, since the dealer must peek at the hole card whenever an ace shows as an upcard. In Atlantic City, the insurance bet is won or lost after all the players have acted upon their hands, since the dealer is not permitted to peek at the hole card until all the bettors have played out their hands.

The insurance bet can be a valuable option when exer-cised correctly, and the odds and strategies of insurance are fully discussed in the next chapter.

# IV

# THE INSURANCE BET

"Insurance pays 2 to 1" is the legend printed on all black-jack tables in casinos where the insurance bet is allowed. Many blackjack players are uncertain of this bet, both as to its proper use and as to the correct odds associated with it. This is not surprising, since the term "insurance" is a misnomer.

By making the insurance bet the player is not actually insuring against anything. At times, the bettor may be said to "insure his blackjack" and that is the only valid reason for the use of the word "insurance."

The bet is made as follows: When a dealer shows an ace as the upcard, the casino allows the players to make an insurance bet by placing up to half their original bets in the insurance box. If the dealer has 10 (any 10-value card) in the hole and thus a blackjack, the insurance bets are won by the players and are paid off at 2 to 1. Should the dealer not have 10 in the hole, there is no blackjack and the insurance bets are lost by the players.

So, really, this is not an insurance bet at all, but a "blackjack bet," for the players, by making this wager, are betting that the dealer has blackjack. That's the only time the players wins this bet. If the dealer doesn't have a blackjack, the bet is lost. The word "insurance" is a vague and incorrect one here, and that's why so many players have trouble with this wager and avoid it.

Although the player may make a bet equal to one half the original bet in the insurance box, the player is not limited to precisely one half the bet. If the original bet is $50, the limit is up to $25 as an insurance bet. Thus, the blackjack player can bet $24 or less or any amount down to the house minimum. But, if the bet is made correctly, we strongly advise that the player bet the maximum, one half the original bet, as an insurance wager.

The bet is made prior to any of the players acting upon their hands. If the dealer's upcard is an ace, the dealer immediately asks the players if they want to make an insurance bet. The dealer might simply say, "Insurance?" At this time the players must make the bet if they wish to.

In Atlantic City the dealer is not permitted to peek at the hole card until all the players have acted upon their hands; the bet will be won or lost after all the players have acted upon their hands. In Nevada, the bet is won or lost prior to any of the bettors acting upon their hands because the dealer must immediately peek at the hole card after the insurance wagers are made. In Nevada casinos, after the dealer peeks at the hole card, if it forms a blackjack, all insurance bets are paid off at 2 to 1, then all the players' losing original bets are gathered in by the dealer. The dealer's blackjack beats any of the players' hands, unless a player has blackjack also, in which case it is a standoff. If the dealer doesn't have a blackjack, all the insurance bets are lost and collected and the game goes on, with the first baseman acting upon his hand, and all other players following in order.

The term "insurance" is more correctly used when the player is said to "insure" his or her blackjack. This situation occurs when the player has been dealt a blackjack and the dealer shows an ace as the upcard. If the player doesn't make an insurance bet and the dealer has a blackjack, the player's blackjack is only a standoff as far as the original bet is concerned, and the player would not win any money despite holding this powerful hand. But, in making the insurance bet, the player is insuring the blackjack and guaranteeing that there will be an even-money payoff on the original bet, no matter what hole card the dealer has.

Here's how this works: Suppose the player has a $50 bet in the betting box and gets a blackjack. The dealer shows an ace and asks for insurance bets to be made. If the player puts $25 on the insurance box, the following occurs:

• If the dealer has 10 in the hole and thus a blackjack, the player will be paid off at 2 to 1 for the insurance bet and collect $50. The two blackjacks are a standoff, with neither winning. The net result is $50 won by the player.

• If the dealer does not have a blackjack, the player loses the $25 insurance wager, but gets $75 for the blackjack at 3 to 2. The net result is $50 won by the player.

Casino employees, such as dealers and floormen, are always urging players to insure the blackjack. "You can't lose," they argue. "You must win something."

The "something" they refer to is the even-money payoff just explained above. However, by making an insurance bet the player is giving up the chance to get a correct 3 to 2 payoff on his blackjack. In the example we showed, the payoff received was only $50 instead of the $75 the player might have gotten for the blackjack. Of course, it could be argued that, if the bettor didn't make the insurance wager and the dealer had a blackjack, then the player would end up with nothing in the way of a payoff, since blackjacks held by both the dealer and the player are standoffs.

To determine whether or not an insurance bet should be made, we must study the odds of the wager.

## ODDS OF THE INSURANCE BET

The easiest way to show the true odds is to work them out with a single deck of cards. Let's assume that the player is alone at the table with the dealer, playing "head to head" with him.

On the very first round of play, right after the cards have been shuffled up, the player gets a blackjack and the dealer shows an ace. Should the player now make an insurance bet; should she "insure" her blackjack?

So far we know three cards out of the fifty-two in the pack. We know the two aces and the 10 (any 10-value card). This leaves forty-nine other cards remaining in the deck. In a fifty-two-card pack, there are sixteen 10-value cards (10, jack, queen, and king) and thirty-six non-10s. Since we've seen two non-10s (both aces) and only one 10, this leaves a ratio of 34 to 15 in the deck; thirty-four non-10s and fifteen 10s.

The insurance bet pays off at 2 to 1, so, for it to be worthwhile, the ratio of remaining cards should be at least 2 to 1 or lower. However, here the ratio is much higher, at 34 to 15, so the casino has an 8 percent edge over the player on this bet.

If the player held 10–6 instead of a blackjack, the same ratio of 34 to 15 applies and the bet on insurance would be a bad one. If the player held J–K for 20, the insurance bet would be even worse, for the ratio would have risen to 35 to 14.

Many players don't concern themselves with this ratio or the true odds. Some bettors make an insurance bet only when their hands are terrible, such as a hard 15 or a hard 16, hoping and praying the dealer has a blackjack so that they can come out even. Others make insurance bets only with top hands, such as 20s. In either case, their reasoning is wrong. It's not what the player holds that matters, it's the ratio of non-10s to 10s that counts. Only when this ratio

30

drops to 2 to 1 or below is the insurance wager valid, and the only way the player knows this is by counting cards. Otherwise it should be avoided. Strategy in making insurance wagers according to the count is covered in Chapter VIII on counting methods.

If the player isn't counting cards, he or she should not make an insurance bet, for generally the odds are against the player. Only when the count gives an accurate picture, showing a favorable-odds situation, should the insurance bet be wagered.

# V

## CASINO RULES OF PLAY

Instead of standard rules of play in all American casinos, the casinos and the gaming commissions controlling these clubs have set up a patchwork of rules, making it difficult for players to know exactly what is allowed or not allowed in any particular casino. In Las Vegas, the rules downtown differ from those on the Strip, and even on the Strip, they differ from casino to casino.

In some instances, the rules differ within a particular casino itself: What is allowed at the $100 table is not permitted at the $2 table. These differences may be minor, but they have an adverse effect upon the bettor, who is often bewildered by the lack of standard rules of play.

Some casinos, particularly the ones at Lake Tahoe in northern Nevada, post the rules of play at the tables, but these are basic rules and don't cover all the possible plays the bettor may make. In Las Vegas, where often nothing at all is posted, the player is in the dark unless the dealer clarifies just what the player is permitted to do. In some casinos, even the dealers are unsure of the rules, because they change often at the whim of casino managers.

In Atlantic City, the rules can be found in booklets issued by the casinos, but the rules are not posted at the tables themselves, and many players don't know about the booklets, although they may be easily obtained if asked for.

Not only rules of play, but betting limits and rules may vary from table to table within a casino. If in doubt, the player should also check these out with the dealer.

To acquaint you with the casino rules of play, we'll cover them from jurisdiction to jurisdiction, and sometimes within one particular area, such as Las Vegas. The jurisdictions covered are the Las Vegas Strip, downtown Las Vegas, northern Nevada, and Atlantic City. The first three are in the state of Nevada, the last in the state of New Jersey, and these are the only jurisdictions within the United States that permit legalized blackjack gambling.

Certain rules are standard for all casinos, no matter where they are located. All of the rules cover plays by the bettor that are covered in full in the chapters III, IV, and VII on player's options, the insurance bet, and surrender, respectively.

Before we deal with the various rules, we should point out that all casinos allow players to hit or stand on any total under 21; to count an ace as 1 or 11 at their option; and to raise or lower the original bet before the cards are dealt.

## LAS VEGAS STRIP RULES

The Strip in Las Vegas is the center of big-time gambling in America. There is no such street with the name "Strip"; rather it is the term used for Las Vegas Boulevard South, running from Sahara Avenue south to Tropicana Avenue. The Strip also encompasses several hotel-casinos off Las Vegas Boulevard South, such as the Las Vegas Hilton, the MGM Grand, and the Landmark.

The Strip is a few miles south of the other center of Las Vegas gambling: the downtown section. The first hotel on the Strip is the Sahara, and thereafter they proceed in a regular procession, many of them world-famous. Others include the Riviera, the Stardust, the Sands, the Frontier, the Desert Inn, Caesars Palace, and the Tropicana. There are other big and luxurious gambling palaces along the Strip, so the blackjack player has a wide choice of clubs to gamble in.

Following are the general rules governing the Strip:

• *The dealer must stand on all 17s.* The dealer is not permitted to hit a soft 17, and this rule is favorable to the player.

• *Insurance pays 2 to 1.* Whenever the dealer shows an ace as the upcard, the player is permitted to make an insurance bet up to one half the original bet. This wager is paid off at 2 to 1, if won by the player. Insurance wagers can be favorable to the player if made correctly.

• *Splitting pairs.* If the player's first two cards are a pair of the same rank, such as 6s, 8s, or any 10-value cards, the pair may be split into two separate hands, but the player must wager the same amount on the new hand as bet on the original hand. If another card of the same rank is dealt to the split card, that new hand may also be split. Therefore, *new pairs may be split.*

Aces, when split, may be played out as separate hands, but only one card is dealt to each ace to form that hand. *An ace dealt to a split ace may not be resplit.*

Splitting pairs is a favorable rule.

• *Doubling down.* On the first two cards forming the original hand, the player may bet *up to double* the original bet on the hand. The player is then permitted to draw only one additional card to the doubled-down hand.

The player may double down on any original hand, no matter what the point total. This is a generous rule and is favorable to the player.

These are the basic rules on the Las Vegas Strip. Other

player's options are permitted in some casinos, all of them favorable to the player.

## Optional Rules

• *Surrender.* After receiving the first two cards forming the original hand, the player has the option of surrendering the hand, that is, not acting on it. To do this, the player gives up the cards and half the wager. This rule is found in several casinos such as the Dunes, the Aladdin, and Caesars Palace. Other casinos permit surrender, but do not post this option or advertise it. This is a very favorable rule for a card counter.

• *Doubling down after splitting pairs.* After splitting a pair, the player may double down on the new hands formed by the split. This rule is prevalent in many of the casinos that feature four-deck games, such as Caesars Palace, the Frontier, MGM Grand, and the Dunes. This is a very favorable option for the player.

# DOWNTOWN LAS VEGAS RULES

Fremont Street is the center of the downtown Las Vegas area, with many large casinos and hotels lining the street. Among the more well-known clubs are the Golden Nugget, Horseshoe, Union Plaza, Fremont, and Four Queens.

The atmosphere in these casinos is more crowded and less sedate than those on the Strip. The players tend to dress informally, and these casinos attract many local people as well as tourists from the neighboring states.

Following are the standard rules in the downtown Las Vegas casinos:

• *Soft 17s are hit by the dealer.* This rule is unfavorable for the player.

• *Doubling down.* The player may double down on any two cards forming the original hand. This is a standard rule throughout Las Vegas and is favorable for the player.

• *Splitting pairs.* Any cards of equal rank, including 10-value cards, may be split and resplit and played as separate hands. If the player is dealt a pair of aces, it may be split but only one additional card may be drawn on each ace. This rule is standard throughout Las Vegas.

• *Insurance pays 2 to 1.* This bet can be made at the option of the player whenever the dealer shows an ace as the upcard, by the player betting up to half the original bet in the insurance box. This rule is standard throughout Las Vegas.

## Optional Rules

• *Surrender.* Only a few downtown casinos offer the surrender option, whereby a player may refuse to play out the original hand by giving up the cards and half the wager.

• *Doubling down after splitting pairs.* This rule applies in just a couple of the downtown casinos, and is very favorable for the player.

• *Resplitting aces.* A few of the downtown casinos, such as the Four Queens and Horseshoe Club, allow a player to resplit a pair of aces if another ace is dealt to a split ace. This is very favorable for the player.

## NORTHERN NEVADA RULES

The two principal centers of gambling in northern Nevada are located in Lake Tahoe and Reno, which are about 40 miles apart and about 250 miles northeast of San Francisco.

Lake Tahoe has both a northern and southern shore, with most of the activity centering in the southern area. As soon as the player arrives at the stateline, there is a casino awaiting. Some of the larger casinos in the Lake Tahoe area include Harrah's, Sahara Tahoe, Cal-Neva Lodge, and Harvey's.

Reno is a much larger city, and is one of the fastest-growing-population areas in the United States. Most of the hotel-casinos are grouped around the main street, Virginia Street, and include Harrah's, Harold's Club, the Sahara, and Fitzgerald's. The MGM Grand has a huge hotel-casino complex several miles from the downtown Reno area, close to the airport. Many other casinos are either expanding their facilities or building new structures in the Reno area.

The rules in northern Nevada are generally more restrictive to the player than in the Las Vegas area.

• *The dealer must hit soft 17s.* This rule is an unfavorable one for the player.

• *Insurance pays 2 to 1.* Some smaller casinos do not have an insurance bet on the layout.

• *Doubling down is permitted only on 10s or 11s.* This is a bad rule for the player and restricts doubling-down options considerably.

• *Splitting pairs.* Any pair, including 10-value cards, may be split and resplit. If aces are split, only one additional card may be dealt to each ace.

The above rules are fairly standard in northern Nevada, although there are several casinos that don't adhere to these rigid rules and have the more favorable Las Vegas ones.

The optional rules in Reno and Lake Tahoe are practically nonexistent, and the best options are available in casinos that feature Las Vegas rules.

## ATLANTIC CITY RULES

At least sixteen major casinos are projected to open in the Atlantic City area within the next few years. This center of gambling is ideally located, having at least a sixty million population to draw from within four hours of Atlantic City.

The rules in the present casinos, and those that will be established in all future casinos, are standard ones; there can be no deviation from casino to casino as there is in Nevada. The rules are set by the Casino Control Commission of New Jersey, and inspectors representing the commission are present in all casinos to supervise play and respond to players' complaints.

Booklets stating the rules and explaining them are available in all casinos, so players should not be misled when playing blackjack. If a player feels that the casino hasn't responded to his questions or has taken advantage of him, he can immediately get a hearing from one of the inspectors in the casino.

In this respect the attitude in Atlantic City is much different from Nevada, where no gaming-commission representatives can be found in any casino and the player is at the mercy of the casino executives whenever there is a dispute between player and casino.

The following are the standard rules in all casinos in Atlantic City.

- *Insurance pays 2 to 1.*
- *Splitting pairs.* Any pair, including 10-value cards, may be split, but *no pair may be resplit.* This is an unfavorable rule for the players. Aces, when split, can receive only one other card on each split ace.
- *Doubling down.* Any two cards that form the player's original hand may be doubled down.
- *Doubling down after splitting.* The player may double down on the cards after splitting a pair. This is a very favorable rule for the players.
- *Surrender.* The player may surrender the original two cards before acting upon them. The player loses the cards and half the wager when surrendering.

No optional rules exist in the Atlantic City casinos, but there are certain differences between the game played there and in Nevada. These differences are as follows.

• Unlike the Nevada dealers, the Atlantic City dealer is not permitted to peek at the hole card until all the players have acted upon their hands, even if the upcard is ace or 10. In the Nevada casinos, when the upcard is ace or 10, the dealer must first peek at the hole card before the players can act upon their hands. If the dealer has a blackjack, all play stops. In Atlantic City, the dealer may hold a blackjack while all the players are acting on their hands. This rule is slightly unfavorable for the players.

This "no-peeking" rule has been put into practice to prevent cheating by the dealer. In Nevada casinos, the major cause of cheating occurs when the dealer and the player are in collusion, and the dealer signals the hole card's value to the player, who acts upon his or her hand accordingly. This collusion is prevented when the dealer cannot peek or look at the hole card until all the players have acted on their hands.

The "no-peeking" rule doesn't affect the players' doubling down or splitting pairs against the dealer's 10 or ace upcard. After the players have acted, if the dealer discovers that he has blackjack, only the player's original bet, not the split or doubled-down wager is lost. This is a fair and an equitable rule and costs the player nothing, nor does it hinder or restrict the bettor's play in any manner.

On the other hand, the player is able to surrender the hand against the dealer's blackjack, something not done in Nevada casinos, since the dealer doesn't know about a blackjack until the player's cards and half the wager have been removed. This is a favorable rule for the players.

• All games played in the Atlantic City casinos are either four- or six-deck ones. No single-deck games are available, nor will there be in the future. Multiple decks are unfavorable to the players, but the rules allowed in Atlantic City are among the most liberal and favorable ones available to players, so the two rules balance out.

## BETTING RULES AND LIMITS

Players can bet cash, but casinos prefer the bettors to use casino chips. If a cash bet is made and wins, the payoff is in casino chips; and if the money wager is lost, the cash is inserted into a slot at the table by the dealer and pushed down into a hidden drop box. This drop box also holds all cash brought to the table by players to be converted to casino chips.

Standard denominations of chips are issued by most casinos. These come in $1, $5, $25, and $100 units. Some clubs, instead of issuing $1 chips, use $1 coins. At practically all blackjack tables, 25¢ coins are available for change and payoffs, since some gamblers bet odd amounts that require payments to the nearest quarter.

Some casinos issue $2.50 chips, which are useful in paying off blackjacks to players who bet $5 because the payoff is $7.50. All casino chips are redeemable by the house for U.S. money at the cashier's cage, not at the tables. These cages are usually located in the rear of the casinos.

There is no standard minimum limit at tables. In smaller casinos and in casinos catering to small bettors, $1 minimum bets may be allowed at the tables. Usually, the minimum is $2 at several tables in any casino, but the biggest play comes at the $5 and $25 tables. Some tables may be earmarked for $100 minimum players. Within most casinos, there are separate minimums at separate tables. Players who bet $100 or more on a hand, the "high rollers," don't like to play at a table with $2 bettors who may be slow and inexperienced. And $2 bettors might get nervous making decisions that may affect fellow players who have bet $500 on their hands.

In the Atlantic City and Las Vegas Strip casinos, there are relatively few $2 tables available. These are usually filled with women, the wives and companions of the high rollers who are frequenting the higher-limit tables. However, beginners and players with limited incomes also go to the $2 tables in the lush and ornate casinos, so there is quite a mix at the tables.

Some casinos allow a high roller to have a table to himself, roped off so that he can play head to head against the dealer. This is good publicity for the casino and a roped-off table usually attracts many spectators.

The maximum limits at most casinos is usually $500 or $1,000. Sometimes, in the smaller games at one casino, the maximum bet allowed is $500, while at the bigger games, the maximum is $1,000. It is rare that a casino allows a bigger bet than that limit, for the casino makes money by grinding out its players and has no interest in a lucky player making a few really big bets, winning them, and hurting the casino's bankroll.

Of course, experts and card counters are not going to be ground out by a casino; these players will find that the casino doesn't really want their business.

The minimum bet is posted at the table, usually along with the maximum limit. A sign may read "$5 to $500" or "$25 to $1,000." Where there is no minimum posted, it is the house minimum, usually $2, that is in force.

Some players like to bet and play out two hands at a time. If the minimum at the table is $5, the house usually requires double that minimum to be bet on each hand. Some casinos have the same requirement for their $25 and $100 tables as well, but usually waive it for those games.

If two hands are played at once in a $5 game, the player is usually required to put up at least $10 on each hand, and

at a $2 table at least $4 on each hand. When playing out
two hands, the bettor is allowed to look at only one hand
at a time and cannot examine the cards in the second hand
until he or she has acted on the cards in the first. This rule
is waived when the dealer's upcard is an ace, and the player
must make a decision regarding the insurance bet. The rule
is arbitrary and makes no sense except from the viewpoint
of possible cheating, when a player might switch cards
from one hand to another, but even that is farfetched.
However, the rule is in force and usually strictly observed
by casino personnel.

# VI

## WINNING BLACKJACK STRATEGIES

If a player wants to be a winner at blackjack, this chapter as well as Chapter VIII on card-counting methods must be mastered. Unless one knows the correct strategy for every hand, it is foolish to play the game for money, for there is a right and wrong play for every situation that develops at the blackjack table.

The strategies presented in this chapter are based on a neutral deck in a single-deck game. A neutral deck is one that is dealt during the first round of play, right after the cards have been reshuffled. It is also a deck that is neither favorable nor unfavorable to the player during any round of play, with equal numbers of high and low cards missing from it.

After we discuss these basic strategies, we'll deal with more advanced strategies, showing how changes in play occur as the deck itself moves from neutral to unfavorable or favorable status. We will also show the effect various strategical plays have on the money the bettor wins or loses, and why certain plays should be made in key situations.

Blackjack is not a static game but a dynamic one, and changes constantly occur as the cards are dealt from single or multiple decks. New situations will constantly confront you, so you must study this chapter carefully, not just memorizing the moves, but knowing the reason for each individual play. In this way, no matter what happens at the table, you will play intelligently and correctly.

Once the player has mastered this chapter, he should read carefully Chapter VIII on card-counting methods to make certain that he knows what he's doing, understanding the reasons for each strategical move so he can automatically make the correct moves.

Since Atlantic City and other casinos are using four- and six-deck games, separate charts follow that show correct play for multiple-deck games as well.

## HITTING VS. STANDING WITH HARD TOTALS

If you remember, a hard total is any hand in which there is no ace, or, if an ace is present, it is counted as 1 rather than as 11. For example, 10–4–A is a hard 15; 9–6–A, a hard 16; and 9–8, a hard 17.

Table 1 shows the most elementary factors in the game and, in some ways, the most important. Unless the player knows what to do in terms of hitting or standing with hard totals, he or she will find it difficult to be a winner at casino blackjack.

All hard totals begin with 12. Any hand below this total should automatically be hit or doubled down, depending on the circumstances involved. Doubling down is covered in a later section in this chapter. With hard totals of 12 through 20 all decisions regarding hitting or standing are based on the player's hand and the dealer's upcard.

In Table 1 and following Tables, 10 = 10-value cards and an A = ace.

## TABLE 1

### Hitting vs. Standing with Hard Totals

(H = hit; S = stand)

| Hard Total | Dealer's Upcard | Decision |
|---|---|---|
| 12 | 2, 3 | H |
| 12 | 4, 5, 6 | S |
| 12 | 7, 8, 9, 10, A (7 through A) | H |
| 13 | 2, 3, 4, 5, 6 (2 through 6) | S |
| 13 | 7 through A | H |
| 14 | 2 through 6 | S |
| 14 | 7 through A | H |
| 15 | 2 through 6 | S |
| 15 | 7 through A | H |
| 16 | 2 through 6 | S |
| 16 | 7 through A | H |
| 17 through 20 | Any upcard | S |

Table 1 can be shortened for quicker understanding.

## TABLE 1a

| Hard Total | Dealer's Upcard | Decision |
|---|---|---|
| 12 | 2, 3, 7 through A | H |
| 12 | 4, 5, 6 | S |
| 13, 14, 15, 16 | 2 through 6 | S |
| 13, 14, 15, 16 | 7 through A | H |
| 17 through 20 | Any upcard | S |

There are three general groupings in the above Tables. The first group deals with hard totals of 12, the second deals with 13 through 16, and the third with 17 through 20.

The 12 is the only tricky total in the charts. It is hit against the dealer's 2 or 3, the only stiff hand that is hit against a stiff or bust card.

All players' hands totaling 13 through 16 stand when the dealer has a bust card (2 through 6) as the upcard, and all

45

hands from 12 through 16 are hit when the dealer shows 7 through ace as the upcard. And finally, the player's hard total of 17 through 20 is never hit, no matter what the dealer's upcard is.

There are valid reasons for each decision. The hard 12 is hit against the dealer's 2 or 3 because computer studies show that the player has a marked advantage hitting 12 against 2, and a very slight edge when hitting 12 against the dealer's 3. However, the 4, 5, and 6, which are the worst possible upcards the dealer might have, forces the hard 12 to stand pat.

The hard 13s, 14s, 15s, or 16s are the worst hands the player can have. The bettor should not hit these hands when the dealer shows a bust card (2 through 6) as the upcard. The reason for this decision and for 12 not being hit against 4, 5, or 6 can be explained easily. The player, as we know, has a great many advantages over the dealer in terms of optional play. However, the dealer has two great advantages: 1) acting on his or her hand last, and 2) if the player busts first, it's an automatic loser, no matter what happens to the dealer's hand thereafter. These two factors balance out all the player's options.

With this in mind, we must remember that, if at all possible, we want the dealer to bust instead of us. Whenever a dealer busts, it is an automatic win for the players remaining in the round of play, no matter what they're holding. And the dealer is forced sometimes to hit a stiff hand under the most unfavorable circumstances.

Let's assume that the player has a hard total of 12. The dealer has 6 as the upcard, and after the player stands pat, the dealer turns over the hole card, which is 10. The dealer now has a hard 16, a higher total than the player. If the dealer could stand pat, she'd win easily. But the dealer has no options in casino blackjack and, therefore, under the rules of the game, *she must hit the stiff hand,* even though she stands in dire jeopardy of busting if she does so. That is another great advantage the player has. The dealer is bound by rigid rules from which she cannot deviate no matter what cards are showing in the player's hand. And the player must use this opportunity to force the dealer to hit first in these kind of situations, forcing her, in essence, to break or bust her hand.

That's why the player holding a hard 12 won't hit that hand when the dealer shows a 4, 5, or 6. And when the player has a worse hand, a hard total of 13 through 16, he definitely won't hit that hand when the dealer shows any stiff or bust card, a 2 through 6. The aim of this strategy is to force the dealer to take the first chance at busting, and thus win the bet for the player without the player taking any real risks.

Conversely, when the dealer's upcard is 7, 8, 9, 10, or ace, the dealer is assumed to have a strong hand, one that totals 17 or more and that will not require hitting. The assumption has been worked out by computer studies, which show that it is to the advantage of the player to always hit any hard-total hand from 12 through 16 when the dealer's upcard is 7, 8, 9, 10, or ace. (We'll disregard options such as surrender for the time being.)

If the player is afraid to hit a high hard total such as 15 or 16 against the dealer's upcard of 7 through ace, the player will be forfeiting many hands, simply losing them without taking a chance to improve them. After all, the player's hands may possibly be improved by drawing low cards to their total. There is nothing more discouraging than standing with a hard 16 only to see that the dealer already has a holding of 17 or more, thus losing the bet without a fight.

There may be times when the player hits a stiff hand and gets a 10 and busts, only to find that the dealer has less than a total of 17 and would have busted with the 10 the player drew. These situations occur, but in the long run, in terms of the odds involved, it pays to hit the stiff hands rather

47

than forfeit the bets to the dealer's upcard of 7 through ace.

When the player holds a hard 17 or higher total, up to hard 20, it doesn't pay to hit that hand, no matter what the dealer's upcard may be. Computer studies show that hitting would be a great disadvantage to the player, for the chances of busting are far greater than the chances of improving the hand. In this regard, we list some of the gains or losses in money terms involved in hitting vs. standing on various totals against different dealer's upcards. All of these figures are based on 100 plays at $1 each.

### Gains and Losses

• The player standing on a hard 12 against the dealer's 2 gives away $4; standing with a hard 12 against a dealer's 3 loses $1.

• The player hitting a hard 14 against the dealer's 3 loses $11.

• The player who stands on all 15s against the dealer's 7 gives away $12; standing on all 16s against the dealer's 7 loses $10.

• The player hitting a hard 17 against the dealer's 7 loses $31.

• The player hitting a hard 16 against the dealer's 10 gains $4; against the dealer's ace, $15.

These figures tell a dramatic story, and that's why the tables above have to be carefully studied and followed.

## HITTING VS. STANDING WITH SOFT TOTALS

A soft total is any hand in which an ace is counted as 11, rather than as 1. For example, A–2 is a soft 13; A–3, a soft 14; A–5, a soft 16; A–4–2, a soft 17; and A–7 is a soft 18, and so forth. However, A–10 is always considered a blackjack, not a soft 21.

A soft hand can never be busted when hit once. No matter what card is drawn, the hand can never go beyond 21, and that is the power of the soft hand. A soft hand can turn into a hard hand, however, after a card is drawn. For example, an A–6, which is a soft 17, if hit by 7 can turn into a hard 14. Or the same hand can draw 10 on the first hit and turn into a hard 17.

When a soft total turns into a hard hand, the player should then consult Table 1 on hitting vs. standing with hard totals. For instance, if the player holds A–7, a soft 18, when the dealer's upcard is 9, Table 2, dealing with soft totals, requires this hand to be hit. Suppose the player draws 5 and now has a hard 13; he must now consult Table 1 on hitting or standing with hard totals, which shows that a hard 13 must be hit against the dealer's 9. So the player will hit again.

Table 2 is useful mainly in the northern Nevada casinos, where only 10s or 11s can be doubled down. In Las Vegas and in Atlantic City, where doubling down is permitted on any of the original two-card holdings, some of these hands might be doubled down instead of hit. Therefore, study Table 2 only if you're going to play in the casinos in Reno or Lake Tahoe. (If you're playing in Atlantic City or Las Vegas, go on to Table 3.)

## TABLE 2

### Hitting vs. Standing with Soft Totals

(H = hit; S = stand)

| *Soft Total* | *Dealer's Upcard* | *Decision* |
|:---:|:---:|:---:|
| A–6 | Any upcard | H |
| A–7 | 2, 3, 4, 5, 6, 7, 8, A | S |
| A–7 | 9, 10 | H |
| A–8 | Any upcard | S |
| A–9 | Any upcard | S |

Table 2 begins with soft 17 because any holding below this automatically should be hit in the northern Nevada casinos, where doubling down only on 10s or 11s is permitted.

### Gains and Losses

All of the following figures are based on 100 plays at $1 each.
  • The player standing on the soft 17 against the dealer's 4 gives away $12.
  • The player standing on the soft 17 against the dealer's 7 loses $14.
  • The player standing on the soft 17 against the dealer's 8 is going to lose $31.

## SOFT TOTALS: HITTING, STANDING, OR DOUBLING DOWN

Table 3 shows the play to be used in casinos or jurisdictions, such as in Las Vegas and Atlantic City, where doubling down on soft totals is permitted. Before we examine the Table, we should discuss some principles that apply to casinos that allow doubling down on soft totals and those that merely allow soft totals to be hit.

A soft 17 should always be hit or doubled down because computer studies show that it is to the player's advantage never to stand on soft 17. If doubling down is permitted on soft totals, there will be several instances, as shown in Table 3, when the total will be doubled down effectively.

The Tables show the soft 17 as A–6, but an A–4–2, for example, is also a soft 17 and should be hit when the A–6 should be hit. The second hand (A–4–2) is not as good a holding as ace and 6, because a hand of A–4–2 contains

50

three cards—ace, 2, and 4—which could help that hand if drawn to it.

Why is A–7 hit against the dealer's 9 or 10 and not against any other card? Because computer studies reveal that it is to the benefit of the player to hit the soft 18 against 9 or 10; otherwise the player may lose to the dealer's 19 or 20 based on that 9 or 10 upcard.

These decisions have been carefully and mathematically calculated: Nothing in the Tables is based on hunches or arbitrary reasoning.

Many players are content with the A–6 holding and never hit it, especially when the dealer's upcard is 7. But the soft 17 should be hit, no matter what the upcard. First, there is nothing to lose by drawing a card to the soft 17. For one thing, the hand cannot be busted. And second, the best anyone can hope for with 17 is a possible tie with the house. Any dealer's total above 17 beats the player's.

In fact, after much experience at the table, the player will realize that one of the worst hands he or she can get is a *hard* 17. It can't be hit for fear of breaking, and the player must operate on the assumption that the best outcome is to tie the dealer if the dealer's upcard is 7 through ace. With a hard 16, bad as it is, at least the hand can be hit to improve it.

Therefore, players would be foolish to stand on soft 17s. Mathematically it's in the players' favor to hit the hand. The move is so automatic for good players that anyone standing on a soft 17 immediately reveals ignorance as a player and is a foolish bettor. There are still players who refuse to hit soft 17s, afraid to weaken their hands. The soft-17 hand is very weak in the first place, however, if not hit. The dealer's total of 18 or more will defeat it, and only the dealer's 17 ties it, if the dealer doesn't bust.

Let's suppose a player has been dealt A–6. The dealer's upcard is 2. The player hits and gets 7 for the hard 14. Now the bettor must stand with hard 14 against the dealer's 2. Is the player any worse off now? Only in the sense of giving up the possibility of a tie if the dealer has a 17 total. Otherwise the player loses to the dealer's 18, or wins if the dealer busts. However, the player, by hitting the soft 17, might improve the hand by getting ace, 2, 3, or 4, and if the player got a 10, the hand wouldn't lose anything in value. In essence, the player has nothing really to lose and everything to gain by hitting the soft 17.

TABLE 3

**Hitting, Standing, or Doubling Down with Soft Totals**

( H = hit; S = stand; D = doubling down )

| Soft Total | Dealer's Upcard | Decision |
|---|---|---|
| A–2, A–3, A–4, A–5 | 2, 3, 7 through A | H |
| A–2, A–3, A–4, A–5 | 4, 5, 6 | D |
| A–6 | 2 through 6 | D |
| A–6 | 7 through A | H |
| A–7 | 2, 7, 8, A | S |
| A–7 | 9, 10 | H |
| A–7 | 3 through 6 | D |
| A–8 | Any upcard | S |
| A–9 | Any upcard | S |

Table 4 makes Table 3 easier to learn and understand.

TABLE 4

**Soft Hands to Be Doubled Down**

| Soft Hand | Dealer's Upcard | Decision |
|---|---|---|
| 13, 14, 15, 16 | 4, 5, 6 | D |
| 17 | 2 through 6 | D |
| 18 | 3 through 6 | D |

Table 4 shows only soft hands that should be doubled down. If a soft hand is not on this chart, it shouldn't be doubled down. For example, if the dealer's upcard is 3, the player will not double down if holding a soft 13 through 16. Nor will a soft 17 be doubled down against the dealer's 7.

The player holding a soft 18 should double down when the dealer's upcard is a 3 through 6. This is a play that very few players make. Most bettors are content with a soft 18, and feel that it's a winning hand. However, 18 isn't that strong a hand when the dealer shows 9 or 10 as the upcard, in which case, the soft 18 should be his against the dealer's 9 or 10.

The easiest way to study Tables 3 and 4 dealing with the soft hands as to hitting, standing, or doubling down is to realize that the worst cards the dealer can show as the upcard are 4, 5, or 6. When the upcard is one of these, the dealer's hand is most vulnerable to defeat because with those cards the dealer busts most often.

Therefore, whenever the dealer's upcard is 4 through 6, the player should be alert to increase the bet if possible. It will be in the player's interest to put down as much money as he or she can on the layout. That's why doubling down is valid even if the bettor holds a soft 13, 14, or 15, which are not strong hands at all. A soft 14 or 15 will have little likelihood of improving when it is doubled down; the logic behind this move is that the dealer will probably bust with the stiff upcard.

Let's show this theory from another angle. Suppose that the player knew that the dealer's upcard on the next round of play would be the 4, 5, or 6, before making a bet. The player would have to be an obstinate fool not to wager an enormous amount. In fact, the player would be wise, if allowed, to bet constantly the maximum wager allowed in the casino if he or she were privy to this information time and time again. In the long run, this player would be a big winner.

That's why, even with mediocre soft 13s through 16s, the player *must* double down, if given the opportunity to do so,

53

when the dealer is showing 4, 5, or 6. When the player has stronger hands, such as soft 17 or 18, the double down is even more likely to win.

If we start with this principle, then Tables 3 and 4 won't be just a labyrinth of figures. What the Tables on doubling down show is: Double down whenever you can, whenever the dealer has poor cards showing as the upcard. Doubling down is restricted with the soft 13s through 16s; as the hand improves to soft 17 and soft 18, the doubling-down chances improve.

It is tempting sometimes to double down on a soft 19 or 20 in certain situations, but this shouldn't be done for two reasons. First of all, these are strong hands that should win by themselves, and doubling down forces a card on these powerful holdings that might weaken them. Second, even if a player had an accurate count and knew the double down would be effective, it still shouldn't be done because these kinds of double downs are never done by ordinary players, and such a move might draw casino heat and reveal the player to be a card counter. It isn't worth taking this chance even in the best situations, for one greedy score might bar a player from the casino.

## Gains and Losses

The following gains and losses are calculated for every 100 hands played out at $1 a hand.

• If the player doubles down on a soft 13 against the dealer's 5, he is gaining $5.
• If the player doubles down on a soft 14 against the dealer's 6, he is gaining $7.
• If the player doesn't double down on a soft 17 against the dealer's 2, he is giving away less than $1. This is a close decision.
• By not doubling down on a soft 18 against the dealer's 6, the player is losing $12.

On the other hand, incorrect doubling down can also cost the player money.

• If the player doubles down on a soft 13 against the dealer's 2, it will cost the player $7.

• If the player incorrectly doubles down on a soft 18 against the dealer's 7, he loses $16.

## HARD TOTALS: DOUBLING DOWN

In the northern Nevada casinos, only hard 10s and 11s can be doubled down. Even though this rule restricts the bettor, these two hard totals are the best to double down with in any casino. An 11 is the very best doubling-down total, since a 10 dealt to it give the player 21, a hand that cannot lose except against a blackjack. The hard total of 10 is the next best, for a 10 dealt to this total gives the player a powerful 20.

The 9 is the next best of the three hard totals to double down with, and this can be done in casinos in Las Vegas and Atlantic City, as well as in certain casinos in northern Nevada.

An 8 can also be doubled down in certain casinos, but although it is shown on the chart, it should never be doubled down, for reasons that will be explained later.

TABLE 5

**Doubling Down with Hard Totals**

| Hard Total | Dealer's Upcard | Decision |
|---|---|---|
| 11 | Any upcard | D |
| 10 | 2 through 9 | D |
| 9 | 2 through 6 | D |
| 8 (5–3, 4–4) | 5, 6 | D |

Table 5 shows the only situations in which a hard total is to be doubled down. If the totals are not on the Table, the player should not double down with hard totals. For example, the player will not double down a hard 9 against the dealer's 8, nor double down a 10 against the dealer's 10 or ace. Why not? Computer studies show that it isn't to the bettor's advantage to do so. For example, a hard 10 doubled down against the dealer's 10 is bad because at best the player is hoping for a 20 and that might be good enough only for a tie. Any lesser card drawn to the hard 10 doubled down might be an instant loser, at twice the bet.

This is not to say that a hard 10 should not be doubled down against the dealer's 10 at times, when the deck is very favorable for the player, with plenty of aces left in it as well. But for practically all situations that come up at the blackjack table, doubling down on hard 10s shouldn't be done against the dealer's 10.

The same is true of hard 8s, but for another reason. Although it would be slightly to the advantage of the player to double down with 5–3 or 4–4 against the dealer's upcard of 5 or 6, it would be unwise to do so. This kind of move is known only to experts, and all experts are counters. Therefore, to do so would be greedy, and would immediately attract the attention of any alert floorman or pit boss. By making this move, the player is inviting casino countermeasures and possible barring, so the move just isn't worth it.

Table 5 is applicable in all American casinos. When doubling down is restricted to 10s and 11s, as it is in most northern Nevada casinos, the bettor should then follow the strategical rules shown for those two hard totals. In any other jurisdiction, 9 can be doubled down with good results.

## Gains and Losses

The following gains and losses are calculated at 100 hands played at $1 a hand.

• If the player doubles down with a hard 9 against the dealer's 3, the player gains $5.

• If the player doubles down on a hard 9 against the dealer's 6, the gain is $15.

• When the player doubles down on a hard 10 against the dealer's 2, the gain is $20.

• Doubling down with 11 against the dealer's 5 shows a big $35 gain.

• Doubling down with a hard 11 against the dealer's 10, a move many players are afraid of, gains $5.

Incorrect doubling down on hard totals can hurt the player.

• If the player doubles down on a hard 8 against the dealer's 7, he loses $24.

• Should the player double down on a hard 9 against a dealer's 8, he loses $9.

• Doubling down on a hard 10 against the dealer's 10 will lose the player $2.

## SPLITTING PAIRS

We already know that all American casinos allow a bettor to split any two cards of equal rank, such as 3s, 6s, 8s, or 10-value cards, at the player's option.

Whenever any pair is split, each card can be played out as a separate entity and acted on until the player forms the best hand, and the player can keep hitting each split card until satisfied with the total.

When aces are split, however, only one additional card may be dealt to each ace, and a 10-value card dealt to a split ace is a 21, not a blackjack. Likewise, an ace dealt to a 10-value split card is also a 21, not a blackjack.

After pairs are split (other than aces) they may be resplit in practically all casinos but the Atlantic City ones. For example, if the player split a pair of 8s and received another

8 directly on a single-split 8, this new hand could be split again to form the basis of another hand (except in Atlantic City).

In a few casinos, aces may be resplit, but this rule applies in relatively few casinos, such as the Horseshoe Club and Four Queens in downtown Las Vegas.

When should pairs, once split, be resplit? The rule is this: If the original split was favorable to the player, then the resplit should also be favorable. In other words, the player should always resplit if the first split is valid.

There are a number of casinos that allow doubling down after pairs are split. In such clubs, like Caesars Palace, the MGM Grand in Las Vegas, and all Atlantic City casinos, this rule is in force. When the player has this added favorable option, he or she should split all borderline pairs, and these will be shown after we explain Table 6 on splitting pairs.

## TABLE 6

### Pair Splitting

(S = split; DS = don't split)

| Player's Pair | Dealer's Upcard | Decision |
|:---:|:---:|:---:|
| A–A | Any upcard | S |
| 2–2 | 3 through 7 | S |
| 3–3 | 4 through 7 | S |
| 4–4 | Any upcard | DS |
| 5–5 | Any upcard | DS |
| 6–6 | 2 through 6 | S |
| 7–7 | 2 through 7 | S |
| 8–8 | Any upcard | S |
| 9–9 | 2 through 6, 8, 9 | S |
| 10–10 | Any upcard | DS |

Table 7 shows only the pairs that should be split. If the pair is not on this chart, it should not be split.

58

TABLE 7

**Pairs That Should Be Split**

| Pair | Dealer's Upcard | Decision |
|------|-----------------|----------|
| A–A | Any upcard | S |
| 2–2 | 3 through 7 | S |
| 3–3 | 4 through 7 | S |
| 6–6 | 2 through 6 | S |
| 7–7 | 2 through 7 | S |
| 8–8 | Any upcard | S |
| 9–9 | 2 through 6, 8, 9 | S |

We mentioned that if the pair does not appear in Table 7, it should not be split. We will cover borderline splits in a later section. There we will deal with pairs that should be split where the casino allows doubling down after splitting; in other casinos Tables 6 and 7 will govern.

The Tables may seem complicated at first, but once the player understands the reasons for the rules, they will seem quite simple.

Aces and 8s should always be split. Aces form the best possible base for any hand, since they each total 11 points, and 10 drawn to an individual ace totals a 21. The 8s are split for an entirely different reason. Two 8s combine to form a hard 16, the worst possible hard hand the player can have. Rather than hit to this terrible total, by splitting the 8s, the player forms the basis of two separate hands with each hand starting with an 8 total. Many players are reluctant to split 8s against the dealer's 10 or ace, but the computers show that it is a very valid move and profitable for the player.

In casinos that allow surrender, however, the 8s can be surrendered whenever a 16 should be surrendered (see Chapter VII on surrender strategy). But, for purposes of this section, we're assuming that surrender isn't allowed and, therefore, 8s must always be split, no matter what the dealer's upcard is.

The other pairs have to be studied. A point of 2s should be split against any upcard up to 7 with the exception of 2, and 3s against any upcard up to 7 with the exception of 2 and 3. This isn't too difficult to comprehend.

A pair of 6s should be split against any stiff upcard, as are 7s, except that 7s can also be split against the dealer's 7, since the hard 14 is much weaker than a hand starting off with a total of 7.

The 9s should be split against the dealer's upcard from 2 through 9 with the exception of 7. Why not against 7? Well, two 9s equal 18, which should win against the dealer's 7, and that's why they should not be split in that situation. Two 9s should be split against the dealer's 8 because each 9 as a base can be a winner if 10 is dealt to it. And they're split against the dealer's 9 because a possible 19 is stronger than the hard 18 the player stands with when holding two 9s.

As for the cards that shouldn't be split, we'll start with the 4s. Two 4s total 8, which is a better base than two separate 4s, which can lead only to troubled stiff totals if any card higher than 8 is dealt to it.

Two 5s add up to 10, a double-down hand in many situations and only a foolish player would split them, forming two terrible hands instead of sticking with the hard 10. Yet, it is surprising to see many people split the 5s. Many poor players, with no conception of the game, think that, because pairs can be split, every pair should be split. That is the worst kind of thinking, and will cost the bettor untold sums of money, because when splitting pairs unwisely, the player is betting double the original amount by playing out two hands instead of one, and will end up losing double the original bet.

Finally, 10s are never split, because they already total 20, a very strong and usually winning hand. But many ignorant players always split 10s, and sometimes they resplit them if they draw another 10. This is sure suicide at the blackjack table, because they are breaking up a strong hand into several losing ones at great cost.

## Borderline Splits

In casinos that permit doubling down after pair splitting, the bettor can split the following pairs, but this should not be done in casinos that don't feature this optional rule.
- Split 2s against 2.
- Split 3s against 2 or 3.
- Split 6s against 7.
- Split 7s against 8.

## Gains and Losses

The following gains and losses are calculated at 100 hands played at $1 per hand.
- When the player splits aces against the dealer's 6, he gains $54.
- Splitting aces against the dealer's 10 gains the player $26.
- When the bettor splits 2s against the dealer's 6, he gains $6.
- Splitting 7s against the dealer's 7 gains the player $29. Incorrect splitting of pairs can hurt the player.
- When the player splits 4s against the dealer's 4, he loses $15.
- When the player splits 9s against the dealer's 7, the loss is $5.
- Splitting 10s against the dealer's 5 costs the player $15.

# VII

## STRATEGICAL CONSIDERATIONS

### FOUR-DECK GAMES

In the previous chapter, the strategies presented were applicable to single-deck games, which still can be found in many clubs in Nevada. Practically all blackjack games dealt in Reno and Lake Tahoe are single deck, and a number of casinos in Las Vegas still adhere to the old single-deck games.

However, the wave of the future is with four- and sometimes six-deck games. There are no single-deck games in Atlantic City, nor will there be any in the foreseeable future. Therefore, the following Tables show strategies for playing four-deck games or multiple-deck games.

There is something good to be said for playing in the four-deck as against the single-deck games. For one thing, even though at the outset the decks are slightly unfavorable to the players and the house has a very slight advantage over the bettors, there are long periods of time when the decks turn to the bettor's favor. When that happens, the player can go on a long winning streak, taking advantage of the favorable count for several hands in a row.

In single-deck games, there is much shuffling up of cards,

often at inappropriate moments when the deck is quite favorable to the players. With decks dealt out of a shoe, the remaining cards won't be touched until the red marker is reached, about three quarters of the way into the decks, giving the player ample time to take advantage of favorable situations.

Often the rules are more favorable in four- or six-deck games, particularly so in Atlantic City casinos, where nearly all the favorable options available to the players are part of the rules of the game. In places where single-deck games are played almost exclusively, such as northern Nevada casinos, the rules are bad and restrictive and hurt the players. For these reasons, many experts and card counters concentrate on the multiple-deck games. These players are not as conspicuous at these games because there is little re-shuffling, and the bets in favorable situations can escalate without the dealer or floorman being aware that the player is counting. Often, they think a counter is merely doing what ordinary players do—raising his bets during a "lucky" winning streak.

## Hitting vs. Standing with Hard Totals

### TABLE 8

**Hitting vs. Standing with Hard Totals**

( H = hit; S = stand )

| Player's Total | Dealer's Upcard | Decision |
| --- | --- | --- |
| 12 | 2, 3, 7 through A | H |
| 12 | 4, 5, 6 | S |
| 13, 14, 15, 16 | 2 through 6 | S |
| 14, 15, 16 | 7 through A | H |
| 17 through 20 | Any upcard | S |

Table 8 is identical to Table 1a, the one for single-deck games. You should also examine Table 13 on surrender when playing in a four-deck game in Atlantic City, for several of the above hands will be surrendered rather than hit. If you are playing in a casino where surrender isn't allowed, use Table 8 as your guide.

## Soft Totals: Hitting, Standing, or Doubling Down

There is no Table for the strategy of hitting vs. standing with soft totals because practically all four-deck games are played in jurisdictions other than northern Nevada. Therefore, the player will not only have the option of hitting soft hands, but also doubling down on them. Table 9 can be used to good purpose in Las Vegas or Atlantic City.

TABLE 9

**Hitting, Standing, Doubling Down with Soft Hands**

( H = hit; S = stand; D = double down )

| Player's Total | Dealer's Upcard | Decision |
|---|---|---|
| A–2, A–3 | 2 through 4, 7 through A | H |
| A–2, A–3 | 5, 6 | D |
| A–4, A–5 | 2, 3, 7 through A | H |
| A–4, A–5 | 4 through 6 | D |
| A–6 | 2, 7 through A | H |
| A–6 | 3 through 6 | D |
| A–7 | 2, 7, 8 | S |
| A–7 | 9 through A | H |
| A–7 | 3 through 6 | D |
| A–8, A–9 | Any upcard | S |

There are differences in strategy between the four-deck and single-deck games with the soft totals. Note that the soft 13 or 14 are hit, rather than doubled down against the dealer's 4. The soft 17 is hit against the dealer's 2, rather than doubled down, and the soft 18 is hit, not only against the dealer's 9 or 10, but also against the ace.

## Hard Totals: Doubling Down

Table 10 is very similar to Table 5, that of the single-deck game. The one exception is that the 9 is more limited in doubling down, and there is no doubling down with the hard 8.

### TABLE 10

**Doubling Down with Hard Totals**

| Player's Total | Dealer's Upcard | Decision |
|---|---|---|
| 9 | 3 through 6 | D |
| 10 | 2 through 9 | D |
| 11 | Any upcard | D |

## Splitting Pairs

There is no real difference between the strategy used in a single-deck as against a four-deck game when it comes to splitting pairs, as Table 11 shows.

### TABLE 11

**Splitting Pairs**

(S = split; DS = don't split)

| Player's Pair | Dealer's Upcard | Decision |
|---|---|---|
| 2–2, 3–3 | 2, 3, 8 through A | DS |
| 2–2, 3–3 | 4 through 7 | S |
| 4–4, 5–5 | Any upcard | DS |
| 6–6 | 2, 7 through A | DS |
| 6–6 | 3 through 6 | S |
| 7–7 | 8 through A | DS |
| 7–7 | 2 through 7 | S |
| 8–8 | Any upcard | S |
| 9–9 | 7, 10, A | DS |
| 9–9 | 2 through 6, 8 | S |

## SURRENDER

The surrender option was relatively unknown until a few years ago, but since then its use has spread, and several Strip and downtown casinos in Las Vegas feature the option, as do all casinos in Atlantic City. When surrender was first introduced, the casino executives felt it would be to their advantage, and it is when not used correctly. But an astute player who is counting cards can turn the tables on the casino and make this option into a very profitable one.

Unlike the insurance bet, a misnomer, surrender is the perfect name for this option. When players exercise this option, they "surrender" their hands and half the wager at the same time. Surrender can be accomplished only prior to the players' acting on their hands. Once players make any decision affecting their hands they give up the option of surrender. For example, after splitting cards, or doubling down, or hitting a hand, a player can no longer surrender the cards or wager.

Here's how the option works: After the player has been dealt the first two cards, the original hand, if he or she decides to surrender, the player so informs the dealer. In casinos where the cards are dealt face down, the player turns over the cards and displays them, waiting for the dealer to take away the cards and half the bet. In casinos where the cards are dealt face up, the player simply tells the dealer he or she is surrendering the hand, and the dealer will take away the cards and half the wager.

When players decide to surrender, they shouldn't touch their wagers or try to remove half of the bet; that is the job of the dealer. Casino personnel frown on players touching their bets after the cards are dealt, for they want to ensure against cheating.

To the majority of ignorant and poor players, surrendering one's hand without hitting it or standing in the hope the dealer will bust is a foolish move. However, there are valid reasons to surrender a number of hands, and by doing so, the player will save a lot of money.

First of all, the worst hands a player can get are the hard 15s and 16s. A bettor should be happy never to see these hands in any single session of play. Unfortunately, these hands come up time and time again. When the player is holding these cards against the dealer's 10 in single- or multiple-deck games, he or she is in a dilemma. If the player hits the hand, there is a strong chance of busting, if the player stands pat, he or she will probably lose to the dealer's total of 17 or more. However, with the option of surrender open to the player, the bettor can save half the bet by not playing out the cards.

Second, once the player learns to count cards, it's possible to take full advantage of the surrender feature. When the deck is very favorable, meaning that there are many high cards remaining in it, the player will surrender more aggressively, getting rid of hard 14s, 15s, or 16s against any dealer's 9, 10, or ace.

Once the player learns to keep an accurate count, the surrender feature is a true insurance option. The player can avoid losing the entire bet in many situations just by correctly surrendering the hand. And the card counter can increase the bet to maximum in favorable situations, knowing that he or she will win most of these bets, and the few times when stuck with a bad hand, will simply surrender it. The surrender option is made to order for the card counter, and is one of the reasons a player should know how to count cards before entering a casino and playing for money. Armed with knowledge of the game, and further armed with the options available to the player, the bettor stands a very good chance of beating the dealer.

However, like all the other options, this one can be used incorrectly. Some players, who don't know how to count cards, surrender all their bad hands, the hard 15s or 16s against the dealer's 10 or ace. While this may be a valid play with the deck neutral or favorable, it is definitely a wrong move when the deck is unfavorable: when there are more low cards remaining in proportion to high cards. A hand should never be surrendered with an unfavorable deck remaining. All this will be further discussed in Chapter IX, the section on surrender with card counting.

Unlike the other options, surrender must be adapted for use in specific jurisdictions. The strategy for surrender is different in Las Vegas than in Atlantic City because in the latter place, dealers are not permitted to peek at their hole cards even if their upcards are aces or 10s. This means that the dealer may have a blackjack without the players knowing about it until they have acted on their hands. Therefore, the players will have to alter their surrender strategy when playing in an Atlantic City casino. The differences aren't that great, for there aren't that many hands that should be surrendered, and the Tables showing this option are fairly easy to understand and memorize.

Tables 12 and 13 are based on a deck or decks that are neutral, or $+1$ or $-1$ (see Chapter VIII on card counting).

### TABLE 12

**Surrender: In Las Vegas**

(SR = Surrender)

| Player's Hard Total | Dealer's Upcard | Decision |
|---|---|---|
| 7–7, 15, and 16 | 10 | SR |

With a fairly neutral deck, the only times the player should surrender is when holding these hands. As can be seen, the 15s or 16s are given up against the dealer's 10 upcard. The 7–7 should also be given up against the 10, because two 7s are missing from the deck, and these are the best cards that can help the hard 14. Since the 7s shouldn't be split against the dealer's 10, they should be surrendered.

Why aren't the 15s or 16s surrendered against the dealer's ace? Because, in Las Vegas, the dealer must peek at the hole card whenever the upcard is an ace. If the dealer doesn't have a blackjack the game goes on, and the dealer, not having a 10 in the hole, could have any other card. Thus, the player has a good chance drawing to the hard 15s or 16s against the dealer's ace in Las Vegas.

### TABLE 13

#### Surrender: In Atlantic City

| Player's Hard Total | Dealer's Upcard | Decision |
|---|---|---|
| 13 | A | SR |
| 14, 15, 16 | 10, A | SR |

In Atlantic City we have a different situation. The dealer is not permitted to peek at the hole card whenever the up-card is ace or 10. This means that the players never know when they are playing out their hands against a potential blackjack in the dealer's hand.

Whenever the dealer shows an ace, the player must aggressively surrender the hard totals from 13 through 16, getting rid of the cards and half the bet immediately. When the dealer shows 10, only 14s through 16s should be surrendered, but even this is a wider range than suggested in Las Vegas casinos.

In the long run, these constant savings of half the bet will add up, and the player will greatly benefit from the surrender option. But remember that the player should learn to count cards and make these surrender decisions only when the decks are fairly neutral. To further understand this option, study the surrender strategy under card counting in the next chapter.

# VIII

# CARD-COUNTING METHODS

The ultimate way to beat the casino is to learn a card-counting method that works. Learning the basic strategy is the first step toward success at the blackjack table, for it will give the bettor a slight advantage of about 0.1 percent or 0.2 percent over the casino. This advantage is a remarkable one, for blackjack is the only casino game in which the player can have an edge over the house. In all other games, the casino maintains some kind of advantage on every bet made (with the exception of the free-odds bet in craps, which is even).

The blackjack player who learns the basic strategy is sitting down at the table holding a small edge over the casino. Although this advantage is rather slight, it is there, and the theoretical expectation is that the player will emerge a winner in the long run.

When this basic strategy is combined with a card-counting method, and the player alters the bets according to the count, that is, according to whether the deck is favorable or unfavorable, then the edge the player holds becomes a tremendous lever to pry away the casino's profits. The casino and its bankroll are now at the mercy of the card counter.

Does the player who has mastered the basic strategy and card counting really have a chance to win? Many players we've watched and interviewed say that there's no way to beat the house. "It's their game, their rules, and a player doesn't stand a chance," they wail. This reasoning is fallacious. What these players are really saying is that they're too lazy to learn how to play correctly. Having a negative and weak attitude, they concede defeat before they sit down to play. Of course, with this attitude and without knowledge of the correct strategy and card-counting methods, they're doomed to be losers.

To answer the above question: Not only can card counters beat the casino, but if allowed to play without restraints, they can damage a casino's profit picture to a terrible extent. And don't think that the casinos don't know this. That's why card counters are barred in practically all casinos in America; that's why gaming commissions such as the Casino Control Board of New Jersey has an official rule prohibiting card counters from playing in Atlantic City casinos.

When casinos are so frightened of card counters, when they specifically bar them from playing, when they get the chairman of a state gaming commission to set an arbitrary rule prohibiting card counters from playing, that's the best proof anyone needs that the card counter can beat the casino and beat it badly.

And that's why you should learn the card-counting method presented here. It's a second step (the first is to learn the basic strategy) toward winning at casino blackjack. Are there any other steps besides these two? Yes. The count shown here is a simple but an effective one, and the changes in playing strategy will likewise be effective, according to the altered count. Still, these steps are not enough to enable the player to be a winner. He or she must learn one other thing, and that is money management, and the self-control that goes with it. When these principles are mastered as well, then no casino in America is going to stand a chance of beating you, the reader of this book. However, before you read any further, it is important to review the chapters on playing strategy. Only after that procedure has been learned so that every move in every situation is second nature, should you continue.

If the player doesn't know what to do automatically with a soft 18 against the dealer's 9, whether or not to split 4s against the dealer's 4, whether to double down on A–2 against the dealer's 4, all the card-counting methods presented won't help. You must know the basic strategy cold. There should be no hesitation about any move made when practicing at home, for in a casino, with its noise and pressure, decisions have to be made immediately.

However, should you think you have mastered the strategies previously discussed and can easily make the correct decision in every case, then your next step is to learn how to count cards.

## THE THEORY OF CARD COUNTING

When computer experts and mathematicians began their studies of blackjack, they quickly discovered that certain cards were more important than others as far as the player was concerned, and that these cards, when missing from the deck, altered the favorability of the deck radically.

The best card the dealer could have in the deck is 5. When all four 5s were removed from the pack of cards, the computers revealed that the player had a solid advantage over the dealer with the remaining cards. This is true because the dealer was bound by certain rigid rules from which there could be no deviation. The dealer must hit any hand 16 or below, and the 5 improved every stiff hand the dealer held. If the dealer's hard total was 12, the 5 improved it to 17; 14 became 19; 16 turned into the unbeatable 21.

Removing the 5s eliminated four powerful cards that the dealer could always use to improve a stiff hand.

The 6s were also cards that the dealer could make good use of, except with a hard 16, in which case the dealer's hand busts with a hit of 6. But the other stiff hands, from 12 through 15, were improved tremendously by the 6s. And the 4 was another powerful card, which, if removed from the deck, weakened the dealer's possibilities of improving the stiff totals from 13 through 16.

Last are the 3s and the 2s: 3 was more valuable to the dealer than 2, for 2 added to 12, 13, or 14 still left the hand in bad shape, giving the dealer a higher stiff hand. The 3 was a little better for the dealer because it improved any stiff hand from 14 through 16.

However, if a number of 10s (10-value cards) were removed from the deck, the players were at an enormous disadvantage. First of all, the players end up with a high percentage of stiff hands made up of 10 and a low card. In these situations, the players are in a bind. If the dealer shows a bust card as the upcard, the stiff player's hand would have to be stood on, rather than hit, and the dealer, with few 10s in the deck, often can make his stiff hands into winning ones.

But if the dealer shows a 7 or higher upcard, the player is forced to hit the stiffs, and take a chance of busting first. When a large proportion of 10s are removed from the deck, the dealer has less chance of busting his stiff hands, and the player will be in trouble most of the time. In fact, when the 10s are removed and the deck gets unfavorable, it is deemed so because the player will lose the majority of hands dealt to him. Therefore, it was apparent that the key cards in the deck were the small ones from 3 through 6 and the 10-value cards.

The aces were also valuable, of course, but they were only four in number and unique in their way. However, if they were counted with the 10s, their inclusion would create problems. A double down of 11 with all four aces in the deck makes the aces into dangerous cards for the player, since an ace drawn to an 11 is nothing more than a 12 and a potentially losing hand, at double the bet. The best way to handle aces is to count them separately and make use of their unique quality. If all four aces are in the deck, a double down with a hard 10 was enhanced tremendously, for example.

But the key cards remain the small ones, the 3s through 6s, which immeasurably help the dealer to form good hands out of stiff ones when they are in abundant number in the deck, and the 10s, which not only make strong hands for the player when remaining in the deck, but form blackjacks in partnership with the aces.

With these factors in mind, counting methods were formulated. A count is nothing more than a mental record of the cards already played out, to ascertain if the remaining cards in the deck are favorable or unfavorable to the player. Counting serves another vital purpose. Once the player knows whether or not the deck is favorable, the bets could be altered accordingly. In favorable situations, it pays to raise the bets, for the player's expectations of winning the hand are greater, and in unfavorable situations, if the bet is lowered the player would lose as little as possible.

Counting also allows the player to alter playing strategy. If there are few 10s remaining in the deck, certain double-down situations, such as the hard 9 against the dealer's 2, become dangerous, as do other double-down and splitting situations. With the deck unfavorable, the expectation is that the dealer will somehow make good his hand, and the player wants to avoid putting out more money when that is the case.

When card counting became popular, when hordes of knowledgeable players came to Las Vegas with counting methods and a full awareness of the strategical considerations necessary to win at blackjack, the casino owners first scoffed at these "systems players," but soon, as their losses mounted, they panicked and changed the rules drastically, in a desperate attempt to stem the losing tide.

The rule changes were temporary for the most part because the majority of players couldn't care less about basic strategy and card counting. Like all losers, they just wanted "action." The new rules were causing them a lot of trouble, so they stopped playing blackjack. Eventually most of the changed rules were restored, but certain traditions were altered forever. No longer were players shown the "burned" card; no longer did dealers deal to the bottom of the deck; and no longer could players raise or lower their bets with impunity, going from $2 to $500 or vice-versa. Since those early days, it has become more and more important to disguise counting methods. This aspect of the game will be discussed later, after we examine a simple but powerful card-counting method that the player can use with great effectiveness.

## COUNTING CARDS

Many card-counting methods are available to the public, many of them sold by mail order. Some are effective; many have little or no value. The valid ones enable bettors to determine the favorability or unfavorability of the deck or decks they are playing against by teaching them to keep track of certain cards that have been dealt out. The effective methods range from very simple to extremely complicated. Some require only a few cards to be remembered; others require practically every card in play to be noted and given a certain weight.

The complex methods can be quite expensive, even outrageously so, and their value often has to be assessed in terms of their price. You might want to examine more complex counting methods once you learn the basic strategy and card-counting method presented in this book. However, no matter how complicated these methods are, no matter how expensive they may be, they will not be much more effective than the one we're going to deal with. We're going to show a point count which is the easiest and simplest way to keep track of cards already played out. And with our point count, not all of the cards have to be remembered—only two groups, which can be balanced against each other.

As we know, the cards that are most important to the player are the 10-value ones, from the 10 to the king, and the lower ones, from 3 through 6. Remember that the 10s cause the dealer to bust more often and allow players to form the best hands, as well as getting blackjacks with the remaining aces in the deck.

The lower cards, the 3s through 6s, permit the dealer to make solid hands out of stiff totals, for these cards, added to the dealer's 12 through 16, often improve the dealer's hand to the point where the dealer will win against the player's stiff hand or weaker total.

There are sixteen 10s in the deck (10, jack, queen, and king). Since there are sixteen lower cards (3, 4, 5, and 6) we have a situation where we can balance off both groups, using the point count.

## The Point Count

This is how the point count works. Instead of remembering that eight 10s have been played while six lower cards have been dealt out at the same time, which requires two sets of figures and then another figure to determine the favorability or unfavorability of the remainder of the deck or decks, the player balances the groups of cards as follows:

Since two more 10s have been played, the count is simply stated as a single figure, −2. The player now knows that this figure represents two more 10s dealt out as against the lower 3s through 6s. Thus, the deck remaining holds two extra lower cards and is unfavorable to the player, for the dealer can make good use of the 3s through 6s to form the stiff hands. Even though the 10s are more valuable than the 3s through 6s, as far as the player is concerned, we give each 10 a value of $-1$ as it is dealt or taken out of the deck. Each 3 through 6 is given a $+1$ value when removed from the deck. We work it out this way because the player assumes from a plus count that the deck is favorable, and unfavorable from a minus count. This makes much more sense than reversing the situation.

When formulating this simple count, we were aware of just how practical it was in actual play. Of course, it would be better to know all the cards that have been played out, for the more cards we can keep track of, the better knowledge we have of the remaining cards in the deck.

On the other hand, the player is at a table in a casino with other bettors; the cards are dealt out by a professional dealer; there is noise and commotion as well as tension involved in the game. For the player to be able to keep track of all the cards dealt out and to work out a method of counting them becomes a nearly impossible task.

The player faces other obstacles besides the ones already mentioned. For one thing, the player is betting with real money and altering the bets with the count, which forces exact and correct wagering decisions within seconds. When playing out the cards, the player must also make correct strategical decisions. And finally, at a table where other players are dealt their cards face down, the player won't always be able to see many of their cards. If the bettor *must know all the cards* dealt out, there will be many blank spaces, and this player will end up making bad decisions, or become flustered, forgetting the correct count.

We write from a practical viewpoint. The most complicated card-counting method is valueless if the player can't keep control of the situation, or if, after playing for a short period of time, the mental strain is so great that he either loses control of the count or has to leave the table to rest. Sure, it's fine to sit at one's table at home practicing the strategy of play and a complicated count, patiently looking up the answers, seeing all the cards dealt, and slowing up the game when there's a doubt about a play or bet. But this isn't the way it's going to be in a casino.

The dealers want the game to move along at a fast clip because that's the way the casino makes money, getting in as many rounds of play an hour as it can. And if a player is slowing up the game by looking around to see other players' cards, or to take a count, he'll easily be branded as a card counter and countermeasures will be taken against him.

It's far better to have a simple card count, one that might be slightly less effective than the most complex one, in order to use it without problems in a casino. There's no use in attempting to keep track of all thirteen ranked cards, when, at a casino blackjack table under actual betting conditions, this can't be done practically.

We write all this from long experience as players: Anyone who's played blackjack in a casino knows that, after losing a big bet, there is a moment of letdown, in which card counts and other matters literally fly out of one's head. The cards are about to be dealt out again, and the player, having lost a really big double-down bet, has to make another one, without even knowing the count. Often, in this case, instead of the correct wager, an incorrect, or inappropriate, bet is made.

With complicated counts, the player is going to find himself constantly in turmoil, losing track of the correct count at the most critical stages. A few bad decisions and the session's efforts might all be in vain, all lost with a few bad bets and plays.

To summarize what we've discussed so far:

- All 10s are counted as −1 as they leave the deck.
- All 3s through 6s are counted as +1 as they leave the deck.
- All other cards are not involved in the count.

The aces are very important to the player, but would upset the balance of the two groups of cards we're following. Therefore we keep a separate count of them, and use it in conjunction with the regular count; this will be shown later on.

## The Single-Deck Game

A single deck of cards isn't always favorable or unfavorable. Many times it's simply neutral, favoring neither the player nor the house. This happens at the outset of play before the cards are dealt out for the first round. The deck also may be neutral during any round of play.

Sometimes the player can get a quick edge on the house by noting the burned card. If the dealer is sloppy or the player is alert, the player can sometimes see the card the dealer is burning at the bottom of the deck. If it is 10, the count becomes unfavorable at once. If it is 3 through 6, the count is favorable, and if the player is fast enough, he or she can alter the bet accordingly, before the first card is dealt out. If the player can't alter the bet that quickly, he or she then adds the burned card to the count taken.

There are various ways of keeping track of cards. In a single-deck game, for practical purposes, if the player is at a table with other bettors, it will be rare that more than two rounds of cards will be dealt. On the first round, the player has a neutral bet out, and should take a count, not as the cards are being dealt out, but after the players' actions have forced them to give up the cards, or any player has been dealt a blackjack. If this hasn't occurred, the counter should wait until the dealer has acted on his or her hand, and then pays off or collects bets for each player in turn. Thus, by the end of the first round, the player will have a correct count.

On the second round, it might be better for the player to keep a *running count*, that is, to keep track of the count as cards are dealt out, not necessarily given up by a player. For example, if a player hits and gets 10, the counter uses this to determine the running count, even if the counter hasn't seen the players' hidden cards. The running count becomes useful when sitting in the third baseman's seat or the seat next to it. In those seats, the player taking the running count will be able at times to alter the playing strategy according to the count. For example, if the count moves from neutral to −4 the player won't double down a hard 10 against the dealer's 9.

In four-deck games, if the cards are dealt face down, it is difficult to keep a running count, for the player attempting to do this will get mixed up fast, not knowing which cards have been counted and not counted. When the cards are dealt face up, the running count should be kept, for the counter is able to see all the cards dealt out and to keep track of them easily.

Let's follow a round of play, at the outset of the game. The deck is neutral, since no cards have yet been dealt from it. The player has a neutral bet out, and will count the cards only after the dealer turns them all over, or when a player's cards are removed by the dealer during the course of play. For purposes of this illustration, there are five players at the table, and we're sitting in the third baseman's seat at the very end of the table.

All cards are dealt face down in this casino, and so, if we can't know a player's or the dealer's card, we will mark it with a ?. First we see the dealer's upcard, which is 10. We note it for playing purposes, but don't include it in our count until she turns over the hole card and acts on the hand. The dealer now peeks at the hole card, but since it isn't an ace, the game goes on.

Player A: ? ?. We can't see his cards at all. He hits and gets an open 6, then stands pat. Since his cards aren't turned over or removed by the dealer, we don't include the 6 in the count.

Note: If we were taking a running count, which we're not, the 10 (dealer's upcard) and 6 would have balanced out to a neutral count at this point.

Player B: ? ?. He hits and gets a jack, turns over his cards. He has busted. He holds 9–6 and the count is still neutral, since jack and 6 balance each other. The 9, as we know, isn't included in the count.

Player C: She turns over a blackjack, ace and king. The cards are taken away, and now the count is −1, for one extra 10 has been removed from the deck so far. We also note that an ace has been taken away from the deck, leaving three.

Player D: ? ?. This player stands pat.

Our Hand: 6–5. This hand calls for a double down, which we do, and receive a card dealt face down. We peek at it and see that we've gotten 7. The count is now +1, for 6 and 5 are easily counted from our hand, since we automatically see our own cards.

Dealer: She turns over the hole card, showing 8. The count is back to neutral, for we count her 10 as a minus card. The dealer starts turning over the cards of the other players who have remained in the game. Player A has 10–4 in the hole and 6 that was hit to the hand, making the count +1. Player D stood pat with J–Q. The count now becomes −1 since the two 10s knock out the plus count. After this round of play has ended the deck is slightly unfavorable, being −1 to the player, so we will make a minimum bet.

Let's summarize the hands played out as open cards to verify our count. We'll have two separate counts going: One is the player's individual hand count; the other the continuous running count as each hand is added to or subtracted from the point count. The = is the symbol for a neutral count.

| Player | Hand | Individual Count | Running Count |
|--------|------|------------------|---------------|
| A | 10–4–6 | +1 | +1 |
| B | 9–6–J | = | +1 |
| C | A–K | −1 | = |
| D | J–Q | −2 | −2 |
| Our Hand | 6–5–7 | +2 | = |
| Dealer | 10–8 | −1 | −1 |

The running count is easy here, with all cards exposed, but if the counter tries to do a running count during the course of a round of play when cards are dealt face down, this player has to make many guesses and assumptions about the cards not seen, which always make a running count inexact.

Next we examine the relationship of bets according to the count.

## BETTING ACCORDING TO THE COUNT

At the blackjack table the player bets with casino chips of various denominations. For purposes of our betting strategy, we won't discuss money values, but only units of chips, for it really doesn't matter what denominations the player is betting. What is important is that he or she alter the bets according to the count. The following is the formula we use:

• When the deck is *neutral* or before the first round of play, we bet *two units*.

• Whenever the deck is *minus* or unfavorable to the player, we bet the minimum, or *one unit*.

• Whenever the deck is *slightly favorable,* having a count of +1 or +2, we bet *three units.*

• When the deck is *very favorable,* at +3 or more, we bet *four units.*

The betting range is from one to four units, not a very wide spread, but effective enough. We must be careful when playing blackjack not to change our bets in a wild or obvious way, for the casino personnel immediately make note of this and will tab us as counters. This consideration prevents us from going up to ten units when our minimum bet is only one unit. Although it would be ideal for our purposes, unfortunately it would cause us a great deal of trouble with casino personnel. The floorman watching us play will sense that we're counting cards, and if we've been winning, that would be enough inducement to run us out of the casino.

It is possible to raise bets above the four-unit stage, but this must be done in a natural and not in a greedy way. For example, let's assume that the deck is +3 and quite favorable, and we've just won a four-unit bet. After that round of cards is played, the deck becomes even more favorable, at +4. Since the dealer placed four more chips next to our original bet on the layout, we can now double our wager to eight units in this situation without getting much heat from the casino personnel because this is a natural procedure followed by many players who are not counters.

Many amateur players automatically double up their bets after a win, hoping to have lightning strike twice. Unfortunately for them, the deck may become unfavorable and they stand little chance of winning the second bet. But for us, the situation is perfect. We know the deck is still very favorable and our eight-unit bet stands a better-than-even-money chance of winning.

What happens if the deck changes from plus to minus after our four-unit win? We don't fight the cards at anytime, and therefore the correct move is to reduce our bet.

We never trust to luck, but always use the count to determine our bet.

It may be that a sudden move from four units down to one unit may ring a bell in a floorman's head as he watches us play. It is unusual for poor players to reduce bets after a win, so we might have to, in this situation, reduce our bet to two units rather than the minimum, just to throw the floorman off guard. When we speak of unusual moves or natural moves, we're always keeping in mind what amateurs and ignorant players do. We have to blend in with them and, at times, adopt their style of betting in order to avoid being spotted as card counters.

Counting cards, once a player gets the feel of it, is rather easy. What is difficult is disguising the fact of counting cards. This subject is fully discussed in Chapter X, in the section on disguising counting methods.

## ALTERING BETS ACCORDING TO THE ACES AND REMAINING CARDS

When a deck is plus any amount, it is favorable to the player, but the plus count should take into consideration the number of cards remaining in the deck. Suppose, after the first round of play, the deck is +2, with three aces remaining. It's worth a three-unit bet. But should the deck be +2 and half depleted with three aces remaining, it's a much stronger and more favorable deck for the player. This is so because not only has the chance of getting a blackjack increased, but the fact that half the cards are played out means that the proportion of 10s to low cards has also increased. In this situation, a +2 count would be worth a four-unit bet.

Therefore, let's run down the ways to increase bets or alter them according to the count and the remaining cards and aces in the deck.

• A *minus* deck always calls for *a minimum bet,* no matter how many cards have been dealt out.

• A *neutral* deck with half the deck played out and only two aces remaining is worth *two units only.*

• A *neutral* deck with half the cards used up and three aces remaining is worth *a three-unit bet.*

• A *slightly favorable* deck (+1 or +2) is worth only a *three-unit bet* when less than half the deck has been used up in play.

• A *slightly favorable deck* (+1 or +2) with three aces remaining in the deck and more than half the cards used up is worth *a four-unit bet.*

• A +3 or higher count calls for *a four-unit bet* if the deck is less than half depleted.

• If a deck is +3 or more, and half the cards are used up, and the player has won the previous bet, the bet can be *increased to six or eight units,* especially so if the deck has two or three aces remaining.

• If a deck is +3 or more and three aces remain after half the cards have been used up, the player can bet *five units* safely, even if he or she lost the previous bet.

Sometimes, the counter will face a dilemma. Having won a previous four-unit bet, this player has increased the bet to eight units while the cards remain very favorable, only to see the dealer suddenly reshuffle the cards. In this situation, if no floorman is watching, the player should nonchalantly remove half the bet and take a chance with a four-unit bet as the next neutral bet.

If a floorman or pit boss is watching this play, the counter may have to keep the bet working even if it is eight units, to avoid immediate casino countermeasures. It's a tough thing to keep eight units on the layout for the opening round of play, but if the player is doing well, it might be worthwhile to do this rather than take the chance of being barred. Some floormen order their dealers to reshuffle suddenly when a player has a big bet out, to see what this player is going to do. The average player usually leaves his big bet out. He isn't counting and is just riding what he considers a "lucky" streak. The card counter invariably reduces his bet substantially, because he is facing a neutral deck. So, in this situation, at times, to disguise play, the counter will have to leave that big bet out and hope for the best.

## FOUR- AND SIX-DECK GAMES

Up to this point we've examined counting methods at a single- or double-deck game when the cards are dealt face down, unseen by the counter, unless this player peeks at other players' cards or is somehow able to spot their values.

More and more casinos are switching to four and six decks dealt out of a shoe, and this seems to be the game of the future. Any player going to Atlantic City faces a four- or six-deck game and many of the Las Vegas casinos have switched to multiple decks. However, as a compensation for the use of more decks, many of these games have more liberal rules for the player, such as doubling down after splitting pairs and surrender. And in Atlantic City, all games are dealt with the cards face up, as is done in some other casinos with four-deck games, which makes card counting that much easier.

When playing in a four- or six-deck game, the count is the same, except for two basic changes. First, the four- and six-deck games are slightly unfavorable to the player at the outset of play, prior to the first round of cards being dealt out. Second, since the cards are dealt face up, a running count can be taken. With these two factors in mind, let's examine the four- and six-deck games.

## The Four-Deck Game

In casinos where four decks are used, the player automatically compensates for the extra decks by taking a count of −2 *before any cards are dealt out*. This means that the first bet made by the player will be a minimum one, and until the decks become favorable the bet remains a minimum one.

When bettors play in four-deck games, we suggest that the bet be one unit, no matter what the unit might be. For example, it could be $5 or $25, or players may consider a one-unit bet of $20, and work in multiples of that sum if they wish. Once that basic unit is established, the player should stick with that bet as the minimum while the decks remain unfavorable.

The player must be patient in a four-deck game and keep the minimum wager going until the count gets to neutral. Only then should the bet be raised. It will be raised further when the decks show a +2 count, and will be at its maximum when the count is +4 or more.

If the player decides to bet one unit of $5 or $25, for example, he or she should raise the bet by another unit when the count is neutral and then increase the bets at +2 and +4. Thus, a $5 bettor will go from $5 to $10 to $15 to $20, and a $25 player will go from $25 to $50 to $75 to $100. If the player has won a previous bet and the deck is still very favorable, at +4 or more, the bettor can increase the wager more aggressively to six or eight units, but not more than that, for the counter will automatically arouse the curiosity of floormen and pit bosses if he or she is winning.

When the decks revert to a neutral count from a plus count, the bets are lowered in accordance with the count, dropping to two units when neutral and down to one unit when minus. In order to win at blackjack, especially in a four-deck game, the player must not rely on luck or hunches, for doing this will lead to losses and defeat. The bettor must rely on only two things: the correct playing strategy and the count.

As can readily be seen, it doesn't matter what minimum bet the player starts with; what is important is to keep that minimum wager going as long as the decks are unfavorable. Then the player must raise the bet only when the deck moves to neutral or to a plus total. The betting range is always the same, from one to four units.

However, as explained before, five, six, or even eight units can be bet if the decks remain super-favorable and the player has won a previous bet. If the player has lost a big bet and the decks are favorable, he or she shouldn't get greedy and double the bet anyway. This will cause the player to go on a bad losing streak, for no matter how favorable the decks are, there is no guarantee that the bettor will win the next hand, and doubling up after losses, hoping for a win, is the surest way to go bankrupt while gambling.

If the player persists, however, in this stubborn attempt to win money back, and finally wins a monster bet, he or she will end up being the center of attention and the casino personnel may take countermeasures, even going so far as to bar this person from playing.

### The Running Count

When the cards are dealt face down, the player should count them in the same way suggested for single-deck games. In other words, the bettor should count only those hands completed by the player and turned over by the dealer. Otherwise, the counter should wait until the dealer has acted on her hand, and then take a full count.

But if the cards are dealt face up, the player can take a running count. The counter waits until all the cards have been dealt to the players at the table, then quickly counts them before they've been acted on. As more cards are drawn by each player, they are added to the count. This is a very accurate count, for all the cards are seen by the player at once. Counting this way is of great help when the counter has to play out the hand, for in many situations the running count will cause this player to change strategy when acting on the hand.

Let's follow a running count to see how this works. We'll be the anchorman, Player E, sitting in the last seat at a table with four other players. This is the first round of play, the game is four decks, and all the cards are dealt face up. Before we start the count, we automatically give the cards a −2 count.

| Player | Cards | Running Count |
|--------|-------|---------------|
| A | 10–J | −4 |
| B | A–K | −5 |
| C | J–4 | −5 |
| D | 10–Q | −7 |
| E | 7–5 | −6 |
| Dealer | 4–? | −5 |

Balancing the 10s and lower cards from 3 through 6 is fairly easy when the cards are dealt face up, and we know at this moment that the count is −5. Let's assume that all the other players have stood pat with their cards, and it is our turn to play. Ordinarily, without this running count, we'd probably stand pat with the hard 12 against the dealer's 4, but in this case, knowing the count accurately up to our hand, we can hit the hard 12 against the dealer's 4. This is a correct play. (See Chapter IX on changing strategy according to the count.)

These kinds of situations make a running count effective. If all the cards had been dealt face down and no one hit, we might have been able to make the same assumption about the count, but it would have been an educated guess at best. Here, it was accurate.

## The Six-Deck Game

With six decks we start our count at −3, and again open with a minimum bet, increasing it to a maximum four units when the deck becomes +4. The increase is the same as with four decks; from one unit with a minus count, to two units with a neutral count, to three units when the count is +2, and finally, four units when the count is +4. If we bet four units and won, and the deck is still favorable, we can go on to five, six, and sometimes eight units for our next wager. But we should do this only if we won the previous hand.

Six-deck games are becoming increasingly popular with the casinos. Many games in Atlantic City are played with this many decks. Resorts International was dealing six decks for all blackjack games with a $25 or more minimum, and four decks for games with a smaller minimum. Other casinos in Atlantic City favor the six-deck game. The more decks the casino uses, the more advantage it has over the players and the less time is spent shuffling up the cards. All these factors lead to bigger and bigger profits for the casinos.

However, the player facing six decks can beat the game but must be patient and wait for his spots. The player shouldn't try to outguess the cards, but go along with the count. Only when the decks change from unfavorable to neutral or better should the bet be raised. In this way, with correct playing strategy and an accurate count, the blackjack game can be beaten.

# IX

## CHANGING STRATEGY ACCORDING TO THE COUNT

One of the more useful features of an accurate count is the ability of the player to change strategy under various conditions. The player who doesn't count cards is always in the dark about not only the favorability of the deck or decks, but what moves should be made in certain situations. Knowing correct playing strategy is not enough; the player must also know how to change that strategy as the deck or decks change, according to the following rules.

### When the Deck or Decks Are —2 or More

The following changes should be made with a —2 or more count:
- Don't double down a hard 10 against the dealer's 9.
- Don't double down a hard 11 against the dealer's 10.
- Don't double down a hard 9 against the dealer's 2.
- Hit a hard 12 against the dealer's 4.
- Hit a hard 13 against the dealer's 2 or 3.

## When the Deck or Decks Are +2 or More

The following changes should be made with a +2 or more count:
• Double down a hard 10 against the dealer's ace in Las Vegas, where the dealer peeks at the hole card. In Atlantic City, however, double down against the dealer's ace with a hard 10 when the point count is +4 or more.
• Double down with a hard 9 against the dealer's 7.
• Don't hit a hard 12 against the dealer's 2 or 3.
• Don't split 3s against the dealer's 7.
• Make an insurance bet, no matter what your hand totals.

When the player uses the running count, there can be refinements of play that will turn out to be profitable. Let's assume that the player has been dealt 10–2 and the dealer shows 2 with the deck at +1. No 7s or 9s show among the players' cards. The player should hit the hard 12.

Let's assume that the player holds the same 10–2 and the deck moves from +1 to +4 before it is his turn to act on his hand. He shouldn't hit the hard 12 in that situation.

If the player faces the dealer's ace, takes a quick count of the players' hands, and finds that the deck has gone from +2 to −3, he shouldn't take insurance. If he hadn't seen the other players' cards, he would be bound by his +2 count on the previous round and thus would make the insurance bet.

Many of these decisions are common-sense ones. A player should not only know the correct strategy, but should constantly adjust that strategy to playing conditions. After all, blackjack is a dynamic game in which cards are being dealt out continually, changing the composition of the deck or decks with every new card shown. Even when the player sees cards that aren't in the count, he or she should take advantage of this knowledge.

For example, if the deck is neutral, yet the player sees

two 8s, two 9s, and one 7 come out on the table, while she holds a 9–3 against the dealer's 2, she shouldn't hit that hard 12, even if the count hasn't changed. There are six cards, including the 9 in her own hand, which would have been useful in hitting that 12 and are now played out. In this situation, she should let the dealer hit first, for there is a good chance that, if the dealer holds a hard 12, he won't get any cards to improve his total.

There are many circumstances during actual play where a running count combined with common sense helps the player. If the bettor is holding a hard 10 against the dealer's 9 with the count at −1, he can still double down. But, if he takes advantage of the running count, and sees the count slip to −3, he should merely hit the hand.

In other words, a player shouldn't blindly adhere to a previous count when new cards being shown will dramatically change his playing strategy. Even if a player hasn't been able to take a running count, but sees two blackjacks turned over and a 10 hit to another hand, she should then merely hit a hard 10 against the dealer's 9, not double it down. The player hasn't seen the other players' hole cards, which may be low ones, but she has seen enough 10s and aces leave the deck to know that the chance of getting a 10 or ace on her hard 10 has been considerably lessened.

By being alert at the table, the player enhances the chances of winning considerably, especially in those close cases where the strategy can go either way, such as borderline hands. In the following section, we'll show a number of these hands, and they should be studied closely to enable the player to recognize these situations when they occur at the table.

## BORDERLINE HANDS

Some of these changes have already been shown in dealing with an altered count, but the decisions in most of these cases is so close that a player must alter his or her strategy to play at his or her best.

• The hard 12 against the dealer's 2 or 3. This hand is a standing hand with any count of +2 or more.

• The hard 12 against the dealer's 4. This hand should be hit with a count of −2 or more.

• The hard 13 against the dealer's 2. This hand is hit with a count of −2 or more.

• Doubling down on a soft 13 against the dealer's 4. With a count of −2 or more, this hand should be hit, not doubled down.

• Doubling down with a hard 9 against the dealer's 2. With a count of −2 or more, this hand should be hit, not doubled down.

• A hard 9 against a dealer's 7. This hand should be doubled down, not hit, with a count of +2 or more.

• Doubling down with a hard 10 against a dealer's 9. With a count of −2 or more, this hand should be hit, not doubled down.

• Splitting 2s against the dealer's 3. This should be done with a count of +2 or more.

• Splitting 6s against the dealer's 2. This should be done with a count of +2 or more.

## CHANGING SURRENDER STATEGY

Surrender, as we know, is a valuable option for the player, enabling the card counter to protect his big bets when the deck is favorable by giving up his wager on certain hands, rather than risking the whole bet in losing situations.

## Changing Strategy According to the Count

The strategies involved with surrender differ from Las Vegas to Atlantic City casinos for one specific reason. In Atlantic City clubs, the dealer is not permitted to look at the hole card when the upcard is ace or 10 until all the players have acted on their hands. In Las Vegas, the dealer must peek at the hole card when the upcard is ace or 10 before the players act on their own hands, in order to make certain that he doesn't have a blackjack and an immediate winner. The following strategies should be employed:

### In Las Vegas

• Never surrender any hand when the count is a minus one, when the deck or decks are unfavorable to the player.

• When the deck is neutral or slightly favorable—that is, +1 in a single-deck game, or +2 in a four-deck game—surrender the hard 15s, 16s, or 7–7s against the dealer's 10.

These hard 15s or 16s are the worst possible hands for a player to hold, and should be surrendered whenever possible, even when the deck is neutral. The 7–7 is a bad hand to hold, since two 7s, which can really help the hand, are already held by the player and therefore out of play.

• When the deck is more favorable, +2 or more in a single-deck game, or +4 or more in a four-deck game, all hard 14s, 15s, or 16s should be surrendered against the dealer's ace or 10. With this same favorability, hard 15s or hard 16s should be surrendered against the dealer's 9.

• A pair of 8s should be surrendered against the dealer's 9, 10, or ace, and shouldn't be split when the single deck is +2 or more, or the four decks are +4 or more.

### In Atlantic City

• Never surrender any hand when the count is minus.

• When the count is neutral or better, all hard totals of

13 through 16 should be surrendered against the dealer's ace. With the decks neutral or better, all hard 14s through 16s should be surrendered against the dealer's 10.

• Instead of splitting 8s, they should be surrendered against the dealer's 10 or ace when the deck is neutral to +2. When the count is above +2, the 8s should be surrendered against the dealer's 9, 10, or ace as well.

• When the decks are +4 or more, all 13s through 16s should be surrendered against 9, as well as against 10s or aces.

The rules for surrender are more aggressive in Atlantic City because the player never knows if the dealer is holding a blackjack when he has an ace or 10 as his upcard. By taking advantage of this option, the player is giving up half of a lot of losing bets, therefore saving money in the long run.

When the player has a choice of playing in a casino where surrender is allowed or one where it isn't permitted, if all other factors are equal, the bettor should choose the casino featuring the surrender option. It is very important to make full use of this option when counting cards, for the player will know precisely when to surrender his hands. And if the deck is very favorable, he will have even greater protection for his big bets with the surrender option.

For example, let's suppose that a player is at a single-deck game in Las Vegas and the deck is +3, and half of the cards have been played out. This is a very strong plus count and a very favorable deck for the bettor. Let's assume that she has won her previous bet and has doubled her maximum bet with a good chance of winning again. But the cards she receives are terrible. She is dealt 9–6 for a hard 15 and the dealer shows 10 as the upcard. If the dealer showed an ace, the player would make a wise choice by taking insurance, but now, with the 10 upcard, she doesn't have that option open to her. The dealer peeks at the hole card and doesn't have a blackjack. What should the player do? She must surrender her hand and half the bet. She'll lose only half her wager in this situation, instead of the monster bet she has put out. The chances of her losing are very great. If she hits the hard 15, she'll probably bust, and if she stands pat, she'll probably lose to the dealer's total of 17 or more.

This player has thus minimized her risk by playing in a casino where surrender is allowed. If the situation with the illustrative hand were reversed, and the player were dealt two 10s and the dealer showed either 6 or 9 as the upcard, the player's chances of winning the hand would be overwhelming.

That's why the surrender option is so good for the astute player who counts cards. When it is used correctly, it can pay big dividends by reducing losses and enhancing wins.

# X

# PRACTICAL CARD-COUNTING CONSIDERATIONS

After the player has read this book and learned both the playing strategy and card-counting method discussed, he or she should be able to win money at any casino offering blackjack. The main problem the player will face, besides gaining experience under actual casino conditions, is in disguising his or her expert play and the fact that he or she is counting cards.

Once the player starts winning in a casino, and wins steadily while altering the bets, he or she is going to be watched by casino personnel, particularly the floormen. These are the men and women who stand behind the tables supervising play in the blackjack pit, the space formed by the cluster of blackjack tables.

If a player is watched—or draws "heat," as the insiders call it—the casino may take several countermeasures to persuade him or her to stop playing or leave the casino. Or, in extreme cases, it may bar this player from the blackjack tables.

# CASINO COUNTERMEASURES

The following are countermeasures a card counter may face in a casino.

• The cards in a single-deck game will be frequently re-shuffled, sometimes after each round of play.

• Hostile dealers will be sent into the game, often dealing at an unnervingly fast pace, upsetting the rhythms of the card counter.

• New dealers will be constantly introduced into the game.

• New decks of cards will be introduced often, slowing up the game to the point where it is no longer worthwhile for the bettor to play.

• The floorman will stand at the player's elbow, watching every move the player makes. When bets are altered, the dealer will be instructed to shuffle up the cards.

• The player will be asked to stop play and his or her name and address requested by a casino executive. A player is under no obligation to give out this information and should not.

• As a last resort, the player will be told that he or she can no longer play in that casino and will be asked to leave the premises or the blackjack area. Some casinos will bar the player from its premises; others from the blackjack games only.

When players are barred, some casinos do it in a very nasty way, sending over security guards to escort the counter out of the casino, and in other ways harassing the player. The player may be asked for his or her name and address and asked to produce identification, which in no way does the player have to comply with. Or the player may, in extreme cases, be threatened with criminal trespass.

Unfortunately, the courts have upheld the right of casinos

to bar card counters. With this power granted them, casinos are not only barring counters, but any new players who win constantly at the tables, whether by luck or otherwise. In addition to card counters, many lucky players have found themselves barred or harassed by greedy casino executives. It's an unfair situation, but the courts have continually taken the side of the casinos whenever the case has been litigated.

To avoid being barred or harassed, the best way to disguise one's play is to bet and play like the other 90 percent of the players who are constant losers. In that way, the casino feels that the player has been lucky, rather than skillful. Once the casino executives realize a player is a card counter he or she will not be permitted to stay or play in that casino for long.

## METHODS OF DISGUISING PLAY

The following steps should be taken by the player to avoid being tabbed as a counter.

• The player should never play at one table for more than an hour at a time, no matter how well he or she is doing. And the counter should not stay in one casino for more than two hours, for even if a player goes from table to table, known in casino parlance as "table hopping," he or she will draw the attention of floormen and other executives, who may simply follow the player around.

• The player shouldn't give the appearance of overwhelming concentration at the table. The bettor should act cool and relaxed, and avoid the appearance of always looking at other players' hands.

• The player should act in a casual manner and try to blend in with the other players. The counter should do what the other players do as far as ordering cocktails, engaging in conversation, and relaxing between rounds of play.

• The player must avoid becoming greedy. Bets should never be raised from minimum to maximum, or vice-versa, even if the deck calls for such a move. Increases should be gradual, rather than dramatic. Dramatic increases or decreases in wagers are red flags to casino personnel.

• If a player is being watched, he should change his whole betting and playing strategy. If a counter has won a great deal of money in forty-five minutes of play, and a floorman stands and watches every move, the counter should now make either a neutral or minimum bet *on every hand* while the floorman is scrutinizing this play.

When making minimum wagers while being watched, the counter should sacrifice a few hands to absolutely bad plays, such as standing on soft 17s and hitting bust hands against dealer's stiff upcards.

• If a counter is being watched and has made a big bet in anticipation of a favorable round of cards, only to see the dealer suddenly reshuffle the cards (perhaps to test the player), the counter will have to leave that big bet out and not touch it. Taking it down will be a clear signal that the player is a counter.

On the first round of play in a single-deck game, the player has a very slight edge on the house, and must do the best he or she can to salvage that big bet. Usually, when a floorman sees the player keeping the big bet out for the first round of play, win or lose, he will stop watching the player, thinking that the bettor isn't counting cards.

• The player shouldn't sit in the third-base seat, but should sit close to it. Third basemen are always watched because most floormen believe all counters prefer to sit there. Also, it is the easiest spot to watch, since a floorman can simply stand at the player's elbow when the player is in the end seat.

• Although the counter will always prefer to play "head to head" against the dealer, that is, with no other players at the table, this is not always possible, and often, a single player draws the attention of the floorman. Therefore, the counter should play with other players at the table, but never more than two others, otherwise they will take away too many good cards when the deck is very favorable.

• The player should be friendly with and tip the dealer at opportune times. Treating the dealer like an enemy makes even an indifferent dealer try to take countermeasures against a counter.

## TIPPING A DEALER

In casino parlance, tipping is called "toking" and the term used in clubs is "toking a dealer." We'll use tip and toke interchangeably.

Dealers make very little as a basic salary; they earn from $25 to $35 a day. Most dealers make the greater part of their income from tokes given to them by players.

If a dealer is friendly and courteous, he or she should be tipped by the player, whether or not the player wins at the table. Of course, if a player is a big winner, he or she should give bigger tips. If a player loses, he or she should tip anyway to establish good relations with the dealers in that casino.

In practically all casinos, the tips given to one dealer are shared with all dealers on that particular shift. This is an equitable division as far as the dealers are concerned, because some dealers may work at a $2 table and others at a $100 table, and of course, the dealer at the $100 table is going to make more in the way of tokes. It is inequitable, however, as far as the player is concerned, because some dealers are incompetent and hostile, yet they end up getting the same proportion of tips that friendly and competent dealers receive. But this is an established practice and won't be changed to please any individual player.

There are several ways a dealer can be tipped, but we're going to mention only the best ways, those that will benefit the player most.

• A tip should be bet for the dealer, not given directly to him or her. If the bet wins, the dealer gets double the player's bet, without the player expending more money.

• In northern Nevada casinos, where dealers are able to parlay their bets after winning, the tip should be placed in the insurance box as a bet for the dealer. If it wins, the bet can be parlayed, and if it wins again, it can be taken down and given to the dealer.

• In Las Vegas casinos, when playing against a single-deck game, the bet for the dealer should be made in the player's betting box, for it can be parlayed there. Once it is made outside the betting box, the dealer, if the bet won, will have to take it down.

• When playing against a single deck in Las Vegas, the player should make the tipping bet only when the deck is very favorable and the player has a big bet out for himself. In this way, the dealer will not reshuffle the cards but deal another round, hoping to win his or her own bet.

If the dealer does reshuffle at this inopportune moment, the bet should be taken down on his or her behalf, until the dealer gets the message. In this way, whenever the dealer sees a big bet out for him or her, he or she will continue to deal the cards.

• In Atlantic City, where only multiple decks in shoes are used and the dealer has no option to reshuffle, the player is better off toking the dealer by making a bet for him or her after the player has won a big bet or had a blackjack dealt. This is normally done by other players. This same procedure should be followed at times in both the Las Vegas and northern Nevada casinos, for it is a more natural one than betting for the dealer when the deck is favorable. By following the normal customs, the counter will blend in with the other players at the table.

Following these procedures will reap dividends in goodwill and decks dealt down as far as possible when the cards and count are in the player's favor.

# XI

# MONEY MANAGEMENT

Money management often makes the difference between a player ending up a winner or a loser. Many bettors know correct playing strategy and know how to count cards, yet they can't win at the game. They haven't learned how to manage their money, or bankroll, and that's what this chapter will teach the player to do. It is just as important to learn how to control one's bankroll as it is to count cards or play correctly, and that's why you should read this chapter as carefully as the previous chapters.

Money management can be divided into several aspects:
- The complete bankroll
- The single-table bankroll
- Loss limits
- Win limits and goals

## THE COMPLETE BANKROLL

There are two basic rules of gambling that players must follow; otherwise they'll be in serious trouble. The first rule, and most important, is: *Players shouldn't gamble with money they can't afford to lose.* A bettor should only play with money that isn't put aside for necessities, such as medical expenses, food, rent, or education, among other things.

The second rule is: *Players shouldn't play with scared money.* Scared money can be simply defined as money that is inadequate for playing purposes. Just as businesses that are undercapitalized usually end up in bankruptcy, so most players who don't have enough of a bankroll to hit the tables end up as losers, no matter what their skill.

What is a sufficient bankroll? The answer isn't that simple, but we suggest enough money to play even if players lose everything they have at three to five tables in succession. While this event is unlikely, it can happen, and if players want to make money at blackjack, they must keep enough cash in reserve to overcome temporary losses. Eventually, the tide will turn and they'll be winners, but blackjack does have an element of chance involved in the game and even the best players in the world have encountered losing streaks, no matter how well they played.

Therefore, the rule is this:

• If the player is going to spend one day in a gambling casino, he or she should have between five and seven times the single-table bankroll.

• For any longer period of time, the bettor should have between seven and ten times the single-table bankroll in reserve.

This bankroll will vary, depending on the limits the bettor is comfortable with. Certainly the player at the $25 limit game is going to need more money than the player at the $5 minimum table.

Anyone can take a certain amount of cash to a casino and play. However, the amount one takes determines the game one plays comfortably. A bettor who brings $100 to the casino would be foolish to play at a $25 minimum table. He'd be playing with "scared" money. Even a $5 table would be too rich for him, because he could easily lose that

$100 quickly, if the cards go against him, and after a half hour, he could find himself without funds.

Therefore, the player should move on to the single-table bankroll, and then apply the formulas we suggest in this section to the appropriate amounts.

## THE SINGLE-TABLE BANKROLL

We suggest that players have 50 times the minimum bet in reserve at any table they play at. If they lose 40 of the 50 units, the players should leave the table. To be comfortable, they should have $250 if playing at a $5 minimum table, and $1,250 if playing at a $25 table. We're assuming that wagers are two units as the neutral bet, following our betting methods according to the count in each situation.

Why should players leave when losing 40 units? Sometimes players will face a single deck or multiple decks that are composed in such a way as to cause them to constantly lose the bets. No matter how intelligently bettors play, they'll be getting a load of stiff hands because the cards are in a definite pattern of 10, low, and there will be no way to break the pattern.

Players facing these cards will find themselves losers. Rather than lose everything at the table, they should leave with at least 10 units and go to another table.

At a $100 table minimum, players should be prepared to have $5,000 in reserve for that game. This is not to say that they'll lose that amount, which is very unlikely, but they'll have more confidence with sufficient money available.

We are giving the maximum amounts necessary as reserves. The very minimum we suggest is 40 units in case of a bad run at the table.

What players might find, using our methods of counting and play, is that they will start winning and end up winning at practically every table they play at. That's wonderful, but the reserve still should be there. Having money put aside this way doesn't force the players to lose it.

Knowing the single-table bankroll enables players to know just how much to take in reserve for the complete bankroll, if that section and our formulas are reviewed. The total bankroll may seem like a lot, but if players are going to bet seriously, they must expect both wins and losses, and losses may run in streaks. With this kind of bankroll available, players can weather any storm and come out ahead.

What if a player brings a certain amount to the casino, such as $500 or $1,000 as the complete bankroll? What games should this bettor play then? Since he'll need a minimum of 40 units at any table, and a minimum of five times that amount for his total bankroll, a player bringing $500 to a casino would have to play at a $2 game. A $2 minimum game requires at least $400 in reserves for a day's play. A $5 game requires at least $1,000 in reserves, and a $25 game at least $5,000 in reserve.

This is a general guideline. A player may take $1,000 with her to a casino and play in a $25 game and hope she starts off well in order to continue playing for the entire day. However, a short losing streak will knock her out of contention, for, if the player loses $500 at the first table she plays at (which is not a farfetched amount), she'll really be playing with scared money.

Playing blackjack seriously should be the goal of every player. And the bettor should play to win, not for thrills alone. Following our money management formulas is the final step toward making a lot of money at the game.

## LOSS LIMITS

The simple rule is this: *Players should never lose more than they brought to the table.* Managing money correctly, players will bring between 40 and 50 units of the minimum wager with them when they sit down to play. If they bring 50 units, and lose 40, they should go to another table or stop playing for a while. If players bring 40 units, they should play them out if they lose all the units, then leave the table or rest for a period of time.

If a bettor never reaches into his pocket for more money after he's lost his table bankroll, he'll never be a big loser. He won't be fighting the cards at one table to his own detriment. The big losers are those who are wiped out at one table, who constantly stay there and hope the cards will change. They don't understand that the first loss is the cheapest.

And *never, never* take out more money and start increasing bets when losing in a frantic effort to break even. This is the surest way to doom and bankruptcy.

If you follow the simple rules suggested here you, the reader, will be smarter than 90 percent of the players who bet on this game.

## WIN LIMITS AND GOALS

Most of the time, the card counters will be winners at the table, but they must know how to handle the wins, just as they must prepare for losses.

The first goal of any counter should be *to double his original stake*. If the player brings 50 units he should endeavor to turn these into 100. When he arrives at this goal, it would be wise for him to leave the table. Hitting and running in this manner means survival in the casino, and less likelihood of the casino executives spotting the expert as a card counter.

But it isn't always possible to win that much. Most of the time the wins will be smaller. Therefore, the next goal is to *leave the table a winner*. To do this, a counter should be content with smaller wins, which add up rapidly and increase the player's bankroll considerably. Eventually, the player will find that he or she is playing solely with the casino's money and only risking their cash whenever at the table. That's an ideal situation.

Assuming that the player is ahead, he or she should start thinking of leaving the table when winning at least 20 units. The player should either put aside 10 of those units mentally or move them to one side on the layout, and play out the rest. If a losing streak ensues, the bettor should then get up and leave the table with 10 units in profits. If, however, a winning streak develops, then the player should put aside thirty units with the intention of leaving with 20 units' profits, and so on, until 50 units are won. When that occurs, the player simply leaves the table. Hit and run: the secret of successful blackjack.

Using this method ensures many wins of moderate amounts, but moderate wins add up to big wins. And it is better to win 10 units than to play on stupidly, as most blackjack gamblers do, losing the 10 units and then going down the drain and eventually losing their entire table bankroll, finally dragging more money out of their pockets. Practically speaking, the methods we advocate not only enable you to end up as a big winner overall, but also radically decrease the chances of your being spotted as a card counter. In this way, you, the reader of this book, having studied and mastered all the principles of play and money management we've outlined, will always be in a position to tap the casino bankroll and make it your own.

# GLOSSARY OF CASINO BLACKJACK TERMS

**Anchorman** See **Third baseman**.

**Bar a player** The banning of a player from the casino's black-jack tables, when the casino executives feel that the bettor is a card counter.

**Blackjack** 1. The name of the card game, also called Twenty-one. 2. An immediate winning hand, dealt as the original two cards, consisting of an ace and a 10-value card.

**Break the deck** See **Shuffle up**.

**Burn a card** The removal of the top card from a deck or number of decks by the dealer, which card is either placed at the bottom of a deck face up, or put to one side as the first card filling a separate plastic holder.

**Bust; To bust a hand** To draw a card that puts the total of the hand over 21, so that the holding is an immediate loser.

**Bust card** The cards 2, 3, 4, 5, and 6, usually designated as such when showing as the dealer's upcard.

**Bust hand** A hand held by the dealer or player with a total of 12 to 16, in danger of being busted if another card is drawn to the hand.

**Card counter** A player, usually an expert, who has a method of mentally keeping track of the cards as they are dealt and played out, so that he can ascertain if the remaining composition of the deck or decks is favorable or unfavorable to him.

**Counting cards** Remembering the cards already played out, usually in some ratio, either a point or 10 count, in order to determine if the remaining cards are favorable or unfavorable to the player.

**Dealer** The casino employee, in charge of the blackjack game, who deals out the cards, collects losing wagers, and pays off winning bets.

**Deck** The standard 52-card pack of cards the game is played with.

**Double down** The doubling of the original bet by the player, at his or her option, by facing up the original hand and adding sufficient chips to make the wager twice its total.

**Draw; Draw a card** See **Hit**.

**Favorable deck** A deck that is in favor of the player as a result of the remaining composition of the cards.

**First baseman** The player occupying the first seat at the blackjack table, and who is the first bettor to act upon his or her hand.

**Hand** 1. The final total of the cards either the dealer or player stands with. 2. The total of the first two cards dealt either to the dealer or the player.

**Hard total** Any total which is counted without an ace appearing in the hand, or, if there is an ace forming the total, a hand where the ace counts as only one point, such as 9–7–A.

**Hit** The act of drawing a card to the original hand of two cards, or drawing a card to a hand totaling less than 21.

**Hit me** A term used by bettors indicating that they wish to draw another card to their hand. In single-deck games this is signaled by the player scraping the original cards on the table. In multiple-deck games where cards are dealt open, this is done by pointing to the original hand.

**Holding** See **Hand**.

**Hole card** One of the two cards forming the dealer's original hand, which is dealt face down.

**Insurance** A bet that can be made by any player when the dealer shows an ace as the upcard. This bet is optional and is won if the dealer has a blackjack.

**Multiple deck** The use of more than one deck of cards in a blackjack game.

**Natural** A hand consisting of an ace and a 10-value card, forming a blackjack.

**Push** See **Standoff.**

**Round; Round of play** A complete cycle of play in which the players and the dealers have been dealt their cards, have acted upon their hands, and all bets have been collected or paid off.

**Shoe** A rectangular box that holds multiple decks of cards, so that one card at a time can be removed easily by the dealer and given to the players.

**Shuffle up** The random mixing of the cards by the dealer prior to dealing them out on the first round of play. Also known as **Breaking the deck.**

**Single-deck game** A game in which only one deck of cards is dealt out.

**Soft hand; Soft total** Any holding in which the total value is determined by counting the ace as an 11. For example, a hand consisting of an A–7 is a soft 18.

**Splitting pairs** The separation of two cards of equal rank, such as 9s, so that each 9 forms the basis of a separate hand, which is bet on in the same amount as the original holding. All 10-value cards are considered pairs for the purpose of splitting cards.

**Standoff** A tie between the dealer and player, in which both have identical totals or blackjacks, with neither side winning the bet.

**Stand pat** The refusal to hit or draw a card to a player's hand.

**Stiff; Stiff card** A 2, 3, 4, 5, or 6.

**Stiff hand** A hand consisting of 12 to 16 points as a hard total, which cannot be hit without possibly busting.

**Ten-value card** The 10, jack, queen, and king, each of which has a total value of 10 points.

**Third baseman** The player who occupies the last seat at the blackjack table; who acts upon his cards last. Also known as **Anchorman.**

**Tie** See **Standoff.**

**Tip or toke** A gratuity given to a dealer by a player.

**Unfavorable deck** The remaining composition of a deck or decks which is not favorable to the player.

**Upcard** The card making up half of the dealer's original holding, which is dealt face up and can be seen by the players.